W9-BDG-625

James McNair's
RICE
Cookbook

Photography by Patricia Brabant

Chronicle Books • San Francisco

Copyright © 1988 by James McNair.
All rights reserved. No portion of this book may
be reproduced by any means without permission
in writing from the publisher.

Printed in Japan

Library of Congress
Cataloging-in Publication Data
McNair, James K.
[Rice cookbook]
James McNair's Rice Cookbook
/James McNair;
photography by Patricia Brabant.
p. cm.
Includes index.
ISBN 0-87701-525-2
ISBN 0-87701-519-8 (pbk.)
1. Cookery (Rice) I. Title.
TX809.R5M36 1988
641.6'318—dc19
88-21154 CIP

Distributed in Canada by
Raincoast Books
112 East Third Avenue
Vancouver, British Columbia V5T 1C8

10 9 8 7 6 5 4 3 2 1

Chronicle Books
275 Fifth Street
San Francisco, California 94103

For Zohn Artman, Jay Baughman, Jack Conybear, Gene Davis, Donald Donegan, Ron Dykstra, John Easton, Stewart Jackson, Daniel Katz, Leonard Matlovich, Roger McCraw, Paul Miller, James Palmer, Kap Pischel, Peter Pischel, Ted Richardson, Jon Sims, Bob Springman, Julian Turk, Tom Waddell, Ian Wall and Bill Whiteside. Each of these brave men touched my life in an important way—several were among the most valued friends of my life, some were coworkers, others were relatives of people I love, and a couple were part of my extended family. They all died far too young.

A portion of the author's earnings from this book will be donated to the feeding and personal care of people with AIDS.

Produced by The Rockpile Press, San Francisco and Lake Tahoe

Art direction, prop and food styling and book design by James McNair

Editorial production assistance by Lin Cotton

Studio kitchen assistance by Gail High

Photography assistance by Edy Owen

Typography and mechanical production by Cleve Gallat and Peter Linato of CTA Graphics

CONTENTS

All china, crystal, silver, and linens that appear in this book have been graciously provided by Gump's.

PERFECT RICE

INTRODUCTION

*F*rom the time I could hold a spoon, rice was a favorite food. Our family in north Louisiana enjoyed rice several times a week, usually covered with some sort of rich meat sauce. I often get cravings for my mother's very dark, rich gravy—made from slowly braised wild duck—spooned over mountains of white rice.

Many miles and years away from Louisiana and in spite of my dedication to fresh foods and good nutrition, I still relish another of my mother's rice dishes, a mushy casserole for which almost every good Southern cook has a recipe. Mother sautéed a chopped onion in a stick of margarine (or rather oleo, as it is called in the Deep South), then combined it with a couple of cups of cooked rice, a bunch of chopped cooked broccoli, a can of cream of mushroom soup, and a large jar of imitation cheese spread. This creamy concoction was then baked in the oven for about three-quarters of an hour and served at home along with roast beef, or taken to countless potluck church-dinners-on-the-grounds. A recipe that relies on so many convenience foods doesn't belong in this book, but my sentimental nature makes me regret that I cannot share it with you.

The Louisianians I know seem to eat rice with far more frequency than most other North Americans, due mainly to the influence of the Cajun culture of the southern part of the state. Rice is an important crop there and is passionately cooked into some of the world's most creative dishes.

But Louisiana rice fanciers can't begin to compare with Asians, for whom rice has provided nourishment for about seven thousand years. Since antiquity Japan has been called *mizuho-no-kuni*, or "rice country." Shrines to Inari, the rice god, dot the countryside, and each field of rice is given a name, in much the same way a newborn child is. In China one word is used to indicate both rice and culture. Most Southeast Asian civilizations recognize rice as a gift from a divine source.

Those of us who are fortunate enough to have access to all of the earth's dietary riches often forget the importance of rice. For more than half of the world's population it is the center of every meal, and its cultivation and harvest is the hub of commerce, culture, tradition, superstition, and religion.

Although archaeologists disagree about the exact date and place of origin, they do agree that rice is indigenous to Asia. Recent digs have found evidence of the wild grain as early as 6900 B.C. Some authorities place the first cultivation of rice as food at 5000 B.C. in Southeast Asia or China; others say it all began in India as late as 3000 B.C.

Rice was introduced to Europe during the Middle Ages by the Moors, and was carried to the warm regions of every continent by early explorers and traders. While the Spanish, Italians, and Africans readily took to the grain, the French thought it only useful as a mushy cereal for infants and the British stored it along with their spices, using just a few tablespoons at a time to make a creamy pudding.

In 1685, rice arrived in South Carolina and soon moved westward to Mississippi, Arkansas, Louisiana, Missouri, Texas, and California. Today, the Houston-based Rice Council of America reports that the United States is the second leading shipper of rice, after Thailand. Even though only 2 percent of the world's rice is grown here, we export an astounding two-thirds of our annual crop.

Perhaps this export picture will change, as the consumption of rice in the United States and Canada is currently on the rise. The increase is due to both the emphasis on the healthful benefits of complex carbohydrates and the presence of new residents from Asia. The Rice Growers Association of California recently estimated that each year Americans now eat 12.2 pounds of rice per capita, as compared to a meager 7.6 pounds in 1975. We all have to eat a lot more rice, however, to catch up with the yearly per capita consumption for Asian nations, which averages 210 pounds. For a Chinese, this overall figure translates into 1 pound of rice per day; a resident of Japan eats about half that much per day. It's no surprise, therefore, that 90 percent of the world's rice is grown in Asia, mainly in China, India, Pakistan, Bangladesh, Burma, Thailand, Indonesia, Japan, the Philippines, and Vietnam.

NUTRITIONALLY SPEAKING

Tiny grains of rice are so intensely packed with nutrition that it's no wonder more than half of the world's people are dependent on rice for their very survival. In fact, rice alone is capable of supplying 80 percent of the body's daily requirements.

This healthful grain is one of the best sources of complex carbohydrates, the high-energy fuel that powers the body. Less insulin is needed to utilize the starch in rice than in other carbohydrates, which is good news for diabetics. Rice is also a good source of protein, although it lacks a few of the essential amino acids to make it a complete protein. In countries where rice is the main staple, its protein is enhanced by serving it with small quantities of animal protein or with vegetable proteins—legumes, nuts, or seeds—that combine with rice to form a complete protein.

In addition, rice is easy to digest, cholesterol-free, gluten-free, low in sodium, nonallergenic, and contains only a trace of fat. Unadorned rice is relatively low in calories: ½ cup cooked brown rice contains 89 calories; the same-size serving of white rice has 82. As a point of comparison, 5 ounces of beef steak delivers 500 calories, while an equal amount of cooked white rice has only 154 calories.

Rice originated as a dry land grass, but its hollow stems, which permit oxygen to travel down to the roots, make it ideal for planting in flooded fields, or paddies. Today, most of the world's rice is grown in subtropical low-lying Asian paddy fields; only a small percentage is cultivated in highland areas. In other parts of the world, such as the United States and Australia, rice is sown much like wheat or other grain crops.

There are over forty thousand varieties of rice known to botanists. Those few we know and cook are descendants of *Oryza sativa*, which can be broken down into two main types. The more familiar *indica* varieties are divided into classes according to the length of their grains—short, medium, and long. Glutinous rice, also known as sweet, sticky, or waxy rice, embraces the *japonica* (or in China, *sinica*) varieties, which are eaten infrequently on this side of the Pacific.

Indica crops classed as short and medium grain produce stubby rounded kernels that are very absorbent, resulting in cooked grains that are rather soft and have a tendency to stick together. In contrast, long-grain rice kernels are slender and considerably longer than the shorter varieties. When properly cooked, these slim grains remain firm and separate; this is the "fluffy" rice favored by most North Americans.

Elsewhere in the world, preferences shift from culture to culture and even within cultures. Short-grain rice is the daily grain of choice in Japan and Korea, while long grain is preferred in India and most nations of Southeast Asia. All varieties of rice are grown in China and preference varies from region to region and even from house to house; some people choose shorter grains that are softer and easier to eat with chopsticks, while others cook up fluffy long grains. With the exception of Japanese and Korean Americans, the majority of Asian Americans, like their fellow citizens on both sides of the Pacific, tend to prefer long-grain rice. Stubby varieties that remain *al dente* when cooked are favored in Italy, Spain, and Puerto Rico. As a general guide, choose short- or medium-grain rice anytime you need a cooked rice with a soft texture, such as for puddings or dishes that have soupy sauces.

Some American cooks advocate using only rice grown in the United States, and especially favor the use of parboiled rice. With such a wide range of different rice types available, following such advice would be like choosing to cook only spaghetti from the whole world of pasta. Cooking and dining will be more enjoyable if you experiment and try the type of rice traditionally used in a national cuisine.

I always keep a variety of grains on hand, choosing one that has the qualities best suited to an individual recipe. For *risotto* that's creamy yet crunchy, I start with authentic Italian arborio or California pearl. Either of these short grains also works well for Spanish dishes, as does hard-to-find authentic Valencia. When I want a fluffy rice to be served alongside other foods, I often reach for long grain, especially aromatic basmati from India or its American-grown counterpart, Texmati. I'm particularly fond of the nutty taste, chewy texture, and nutritional benefits of brown rice and, though certainly inauthentic, use it for Chinese stir-fry and with Creole red beans. Most of the recipes in this book can be successfully prepared with brown or polished rice; just keep in mind that brown rice will take more time and perhaps a little more liquid. For some dishes, however, white rice is essential to achieve an authentic character and I've specified its use in those cases.

Rice is so delicious on its own that it's well worth learning how to cook it perfectly every time. The next several pages tell you everything you need to know to cook any length of grain, brown or polished, by several methods.

Perhaps most important to good cooks everywhere is the versatility of rice. First, it is bland enough to be the ideal accompaniment to other foods. Second, its juice-absorbing properties render it the best starting point for a wide range of culinary triumphs. Good cooks in Louisiana, the Middle East, East Asia, Southeast Asia, India, Italy, and a host of Spanish-speaking countries work such magic with this grain that I could easily have written a book on the rice dishes of each of these cuisines. Instead I have gathered a collection of recipes that represents some of my favorites from around the globe, divided into two sections—savory and sweet.

BROWN vs. WHITE

Brown rice is the natural state; white kernels are the result of polishing away the fibrous outer layers of bran and the inner layer of germ. These "coatings" contain many of the grain's vitamins, minerals, and oils, and much of its protein. Because the bran fiber has bulk, brown rice is chewier and more filling, which appeases the appetite more quickly and speeds up digestion. The fiber also helps reduce the potential risk of contracting intestinal disorders.

The practice of polishing rice began as a means of lengthening shelf life. Without the oils found in the coverings, rice lasts indefinitely. Some people prefer white rice because they find it easier to digest. Also, many Asians, like many Americans, look down on unpolished rice as inferior, or lacking in status. They are aware that the white grains have been stripped of most of the natural vitamins and minerals and some of the protein, but feel that sauces and other accompaniments will compensate nutritionally for what is lost in the milling.

Greenish grains are often found in brown rice grown in nontropical areas where sunshine was insufficient to dry the kernels completely during the final ripening stage. They cook up the same as fully dried grains.

The Rice Pantry

For the recipes in this book, I have used only whole-grain rice. There are, however, numerous products made from rice that will add flair to your cooking. Most are readily available from stores that specialize in Asian foods and in many supermarkets.

RICE CAKES. Crunchy light cakes made from puffed rice are especially good for dieters; available in natural foods stores. Very dense Asian-style cylinders should be steamed before serving; they are unlikely to appeal to Western palates.

RICE CEREALS. Puffed rice treats range from the old standbys to new unsweetened puffed brown rice cereals available in natural foods markets.

RICE CRACKERS. Glazed crisp crackers made from rice flour come in a wide variety of shapes and sizes; good for snacking.

RICE NOODLES. Made from rice flour, and available fresh and dried in a variety of widths. Fresh noodles are used in Chinese beef *chow fun*, Malaysian *laksa*, and some dim sum dishes, like *chung fun* (large round rice noodle, like a pancake, rolled with filling of shrimp, pork, or vegetables). Thin dried noodles known as rice sticks (*mai fun* or *my foon*) puff up instantly when dropped into hot oil; popular in dishes such as Chinese chicken salad and Thai sweet-and-sour crisp noodles (*mee krob*).

ARBORIO. This short-grain white rice from the Po River valley of northern Italy is used in *risotto*, where it cooks up creamy yet firm to the bite; similar to the California-grown short-grain variety called pearl.

BASMATI. A very slender, long-grain, highly aromatic rice grown in India, Pakistan, and Iran that is aged for a year after harvesting to develop full flavor. Available brown or white; prized by chefs for its nutty aroma and taste. Texmati is a Texas-grown variety with similar character.

BLACK AND RED. Rare Asian grains with black or red husk and bran coverings; although now cultivated in California, they remain in short supply. These exotic grains are presently added to commercial blends along with other brown rice.

ENRICHED. Labels are required by law to acknowledge the addition of vitamins and minerals during processing. The nutrients lost in polishing have been at least partially replaced in "enriched" grains.

GLUTINOUS. Also known as sweet, sticky, or waxy rice; broad, short grains in white, brown, or black, that stick together during cooking and are sweeter and stronger in flavor than *indica* rice. Eaten daily in northeast Thailand and in Laos, but mainly used to make Asian sweets or snacks and ceremonial foods; good for desserts when you want to keep extra sugars to a minimum.

INSTANT. Rice that has been precooked, then dehydrated; not recommended for people who enjoy rice.

LONG GRAIN. Kernels average about 7 millimeters in length and are about five times as long as they are wide; sold brown or white under American labels that include Carolina, Hinode, and Patna. Also look for flavorful basmati variety from India, jasmine-scented type from Thailand, and wild pecan from Louisiana. Cooked grains are fluffy and remain separate.

MEDIUM GRAIN. Kernels are about 6 millimeters long and somewhat wider than long grain varieties; sold brown or white under names such as Calrose. Cooks up soft.

PARBOILED. Sold under the trademark Converted. Not precooked as many suspect, but parboiled by a patented process that helps retain many of the vitamins found in unprocessed rice, since the nutrients soak into the rice kernels before the outer layers are removed; a similar process has been practiced in India for centuries. Virtually foolproof, parboiled rice cooks up fluffy with separate, distinct grains, making it a favorite of American cooks. To prepare, follow package directions; it can be used in recipes that call for long-grain rice.

SHORT GRAIN. Kernels average about 5 millimeters in length and are much thicker than long-grain varieties; sold brown or white under such labels as Calusa. Grains are soft and tend to stick together when cooked. Pearl is a California-grown variety with qualities similar to those of arborio.

WHEANI. A California-grown hybrid brown rice with Indian *basmati* in its ancestry; reddish color and very nutty aroma and flavor.

WILD. When is a rice not a rice? When it's what we call "wild rice," actually the seed of a plume-topped wild aquatic grass (*Zizania aquatica*) found mainly in the north-central United States and in Canada. Expensive due to short supply and hand gathering and thrashing; extend value by mixing with other rice after cooking.

WILD PECAN. Don't expect any pecans in this domesticated long-grain white variety from south Louisiana; name comes from the nutty aroma and flavor.

RICE FLOUR. Made from both glutinous and *indica* type kernels, this specialty is used in numerous Asian dishes. It can be used in many western baked goods, making it a great product for people with wheat allergies; follow package directions. Brown rice flour is available in natural foods stores.

RICE PAPER. Sometimes labeled *banh trang*, these very thin round or triangular sheets of dried rice dough are used as wrappers for rolled Southeast Asian foods, such as Vietnamese *cha gio*. Before using, moisten with water to make them pliable.

RICE VINEGAR. Mild white rice vinegar from Japan is the preferred choice for *sushi*. I enjoy it in both Asian and Western-style salad dressings. Avoid the seasoned varieties containing monosodium glutamate and flavorings. From China, you might try light rice vinegar (*bok my tso* or *bye mee tsoo*), or more strongly flavored, aged variations that are dark reddish (*hong tso* or *hoong tsoo*) or black (*hut tso* or *hey tsoo*).

RICE WINE. Several types of Chinese rice wine (*shao hsing jyo* or *siew hing jao*) are available for drinking or cooking. Japanese rice wine (*sake*) is slightly sweet and tastes best when served warmed; a sweetened version (*mirin*) is used only for cooking.

TOASTED RICE TEA. For a soothing hot beverage with a nutty flavor, purchase mixtures of green tea and toasted rice from Japan (*genmai cha*) or China (*sao my cha* or *hswan mee cha*).

How to Cook Perfect Rice

RICE COOKERS

Electric rice cookers turn out perfect rice every time and require very little of the cook's attention. Just remember always to follow the manufacturer's instructions. I don't like the texture of rice that has been cooked in an all-purpose electric steamer. Nor do I recommend steaming rice in a conventional steamer, as the necessary frequent stirring breaks the fragile grains and results in mushy kernels.

For flavorful, perfectly cooked rice, the following method is virtually foolproof, once you have mastered the technique. Rice cooked in this manner is often referred to as "steamed" rice. In fact, the grains cook by absorbing the water in which they are immersed. The never-fail recipe on page 15 works for short-, medium-, or long-grain white or brown rice or parboiled rice and can be used for stove-top or oven cooking. Glutinous rice should be cooked as directed on page 18.

The cooks I know are evenly divided over the question of whether or not to wash domestically grown and packaged rice. Even though a light rinsing or a thorough washing carries away some of the minerals and other nutrients, many advocate this practice for the sake of the superior taste, tender texture, and fluffy appearance of the cooked rice.

Until recently, it was necessary to wash all rice before cooking it. Domestic rice was coated with glucose and talc to keep the bran from turning rancid and to give the kernels a highly polished appearance. The United States Department of Agriculture has made the use of talc illegal because it is potentially carcinogenic. Currently no coatings are used on domestic rice, making washing unnecessary from a health-hazard standpoint. Washing is still recommended for imported rice, however, especially crops from Asian growers. Japanese rice, for example, is coated with cornstarch, which, if not rinsed off, results in a bowl of mushy rice. Washing also removes the oily bran residue that can impart a rancid taste.

Select a heavy pot that has a tight-fitting lid to prevent steam from escaping during cooking. If you are in doubt about how well the lid fits, cover the pot with a layer of foil and crinkle the edges to seal before topping with the lid.

I find that sautéing rice in butter or oil before adding liquid helps keep the grains separate during cooking. Use a wooden spoon and stir gently to prevent crushing the kernels. I often add onion because I like the flavor it imparts to a pot of rice.

I usually cook rice in chicken, meat, fish, or vegetable stocks; although homemade ones usually have more flavor, canned broths or reconstituted dried stock bases work fine. For a change of pace, dilute fresh or canned juices with an equal portion of water. Try spiced or plain tomato or other vegetable juices, or fruit juices such as apple, lemon, or orange. Always choose liquids that complement the finished or accompanying dish.

For plain rice to accompany Asian dishes or as an ingredient for sweets, omit the butter and onion and use water for the cooking liquid. See pages 9-11 for choice of short- or long-grain rice.

The exact amount of cooking liquid varies with the type of rice, length of storage (the older the rice, the longer it takes to cook), and altitude (increase the cooking time when you are in the mountains). Try a batch with the measurements given, then increase or decrease according to personal preference. If you like firmer rice, reduce the liquid by about ¼ cup and cooking time by 5 minutes. For softer rice increase the liquid by about ¼ cup and the cooking time by 5 minutes. If you plan to refrigerate the rice before using it, add about ½ cup extra liquid in addition to the amount specified to keep the rice from becoming hard during cold storage.

Once the liquid has been added and brought to a boil, the pan must be covered and the heat reduced to very low. If you cannot accurately adjust your burner, transfer the pot to a preheated 400° F oven to finish cooking.

For more servings, double or triple the recipe that follows. Just remember these simple ratios: 1½ cups liquid per 1 cup white rice, 2 cups liquid per 1 cup brown rice, or 2½ cups liquid per 1 cup parboiled rice. I don't recommend cooking more than 3 cups of rice at a time by this method. Use more pots if you need more rice.

SPECIAL PRESENTATIONS

Hot or cold rice dishes can be formed into attractive rounds or ovals with a generously buttered ice cream scoop. Pack the rice into the scoop, pressing gently to eliminate air pockets, and carefully turn it out onto individual plates. Use your fingers to reposition any rice that separates. Creamy or moist dishes such as stuffing, *risotto*, or pudding or plain rice tossed with plenty of butter hold together best.

Rice fashioned into simple or fanciful shapes will add interest to a meal. For individual servings, choose small metal or ceramic molds, ramekins, or even teacups. For table or buffet service, choose larger molds such as rings, squares, ovals, or whimsical shapes. Soufflé dishes or shallow bowls also work very well. Both rice salads or other room-temperature creations and warm rice dishes can be molded. Generously butter the bottom and sides of the container and spoon in the rice, pressing gently to eliminate air pockets. Let stand for about 5 minutes. Invert carefully onto plates or a serving platter. Pilafs and dishes containing cheese should be warmed in a preheated 350° F oven until heated through, about 5 to 15 minutes. Let stand briefly before unmolding.

Perfect Rice

Be sure to read the preceeding two pages before using this recipe.

If using imported rice, spread it it out on a tray or flat surface and pick over it by hand to remove any foreign bits or imperfect grains.

To wash the rice (see page 12 on whether this step is necessary), place it in a bowl and add cold water to cover. Stir vigorously with your fingertips, then drain off the water. Repeat this procedure several times until the water runs almost clear. If desired, transfer the rice to a bowl and soak in water to cover for at least 1 hour or as long as overnight (soaking the kernels assures a more uniformly cooked pot of rice). Drain well.

Heat 1 tablespoon of the butter or oil in a heavy saucepan over medium-high heat. Add the onion and sauté until soft but not browned, about 5 minutes. Add the drained rice and gently sauté until all the grains are well coated, about 2 minutes.

If using regular white rice, add 1½ cups of the stock, broth, or water and salt to taste. For brown rice, add 2 cups of the selected cooking liquid. For parboiled rice, add 2½ cups liquid. Bring to a boil, then stir once, reduce the heat to very low, cover tightly, and simmer white rice for 17 minutes or brown rice for 45 minutes; follow package directions for cooking parboiled rice. In any case, do not remove the cover or stir during cooking.

Remove white rice from the heat. If any liquid remains in the pot, cover again and place over low heat until the liquid evaporates, 2 to 4 minutes. Turn off the heat under the brown rice and let stand on the warm burner for 10 minutes before removing cover. Add the remaining butter, if using, to the finished rice and fluff with a fork, lifting from the bottom instead of stirring, to separate grains gently.

Alternatively, prepare as above but cover tightly and transfer to a preheated 400° F oven just as soon as the liquid boils. Cooking times are the same.

Makes about 3 cups white or parboiled rice, or 3 to 4 cups brown rice; serves 4 or 5, or fewer if serving an Asian meal.

1 cup short-, medium-, or long-grain rice
2 tablespoons unsalted butter, or 1 tablespoon safflower oil or olive oil
¼ to ½ cup finely chopped yellow onion
1½ to 2½ cups homemade stock, canned broth, or water
Salt

COCONUT MILK

Rice cooked in coconut milk is a mainstay of Southeast Asian cooking and is popular in several Caribbean nations. Making the milk from a fresh coconut is time-consuming, so I recommend you use canned unsweetened coconut milk. (This is not the very sweet canned cream of coconut used in tropical drinks.)

Look for the coconut milk, usually imported from Thailand, in markets that specialize in Asian foods and in some supermarkets. Always shake the can before using, unless you wish to collect the coconut cream that rises to the top. To remove the cream, open the unshaken can and spoon off the thick top layer. This rich cream will also form on the top of chilled freshly made coconut milk.

If you cannot locate canned unsweetened coconut milk, cover 4 cups shredded fresh coconut or 4 cups dried unsweetened (dessicated) grated coconut (available in natural-foods stores) with 6 cups boiling water or warmed milk and let stand for 30 minutes. Strain the liquid through cheesecloth, squeezing cloth to extract all the milk. A less intensely flavored version can be made by repeating the process with the drained coconut meat.

VARIATIONS

COCONUT RICE. Use coconut milk (see sidebar) for the cooking liquid. If cooking the rice to use in a dessert, eliminate the onion. When fluffing, blend in any thick coconut cream that has risen to the top of the rice during cooking.

CURRIED RICE. Add ½ teaspoon curry powder when sautéing the rice, then fold in plumped raisins and chopped chutney to taste when fluffing the cooked rice.

HERBED RICE. For a green version, add about 1 teaspoon minced fresh herb—one kind or a mixture you enjoy—or ½ teaspoon dried herb, crumbled, when you stir in the rice. Vary the amount according to taste. For white rice infused with herbal flavor, lay several fresh herb sprigs on top of the rice when you add the liquid, then discard the wilted sprigs before serving.

LEMON RICE. Add 1 or 2 teaspoons grated lemon zest (without any bitter white pith) when you stir in the rice. At the same time, add chopped fresh or crumbled dried dill or tarragon to taste, if desired.

MACARONI RICE. For a side dish that beats the packaged "San Francisco treat," combine an equal portion of rice with dried thin pasta such as spaghetti or vermicelli, broken into 1 inch lengths, and sauté together. Add other seasonings as desired.

MUSHROOM RICE. Sauté about ½ cup minced fresh cultivated or wild mushrooms along with the onion.

NUTTY RICE. Sauté about ¼ cup pine nuts, slivered blanched almonds, or chopped pecans, walnuts, cashews, or pistachios along with the rice.

SAFFRON RICE. Add ¼ teaspoon crumbled saffron threads or ⅛ teaspoon powdered saffron, or to taste, when you stir in the rice.

SPANISH-STYLE CUMIN RICE. Add 1 teaspoon minced or pressed garlic, or to taste, and ½ teaspoon ground cumin, or to taste, when you stir in the rice.

SPICY RICE. Add ground cayenne pepper or chopped fresh chili pepper to taste along with the salt.

Boiled Rice

Some people prefer boiling rice instead of cooking it by the absorption method described in Perfect Rice. A number of dishes call for the boiling technique because the grains remain firm, which is particularly important when rice will be cooked further in the recipe. It is also ideal for recipes such as Indian *biryani* that call for presoaking the rice to keep the grains separate. Use either brown or white rice.

Any of the seasonings suggested under Perfect Rice Variations can be stirred in along with the butter.

Wash and drain the rice as described on page 12.

In a large stockpot, bring the water to a boil, then stir in the salt. Sprinkle the rice in gradually so the water does not stop boiling. Boil until the rice is done to your taste; remove a grain and taste-test by biting as you would check pasta. Drain immediately, transfer to a bowl, add butter if desired, and fluff with a fork, lifting from the bottom instead of stirring.

Makes about 3 cups white rice, or 3 to 4 cups brown rice; serves 4.

1 cup short-, medium-, or long-grain rice
2 quarts water
1 tablespoon salt
1 tablespoon unsalted butter (optional)

Microwaved Rice

Microwave ovens cook both brown and white rice successfully, but don't expect to save much time.

Wash and drain the rice as described on page 12.

In a microwave baking dish, combine the rice, butter, liquid, and salt to taste and stir. Cover tightly with a microwave cover or plastic wrap and cook at maximum power until boiling, about 5 minutes. Reduce power to 50 percent and cook white rice until tender and all liquid has been absorbed, about 15 minutes longer. If cooking brown rice, reduce the power to 30 percent and cook until rice is tender, about 30 minutes longer.

Makes about 3 cups white rice, or 3 to 4 cups brown rice; serves 4.

1 cup short-, medium-, or long-grain rice
1 tablespoon unsalted butter
2 cups homemade stock, canned broth, or water
Salt

Basic Glutinous Rice

1 cup white, brown, or black
    glutinous rice
Water

Plan ahead because glutinous rice must be soaked prior to cooking.

Wash and drain the rice as described on page 12.

Place the rice in a bowl and add enough water to immerse the rice completely. Soak at least 4 hours or, preferably, as long as overnight. Drain.

Line a steamer basket or colander with moistened cheesecloth. (This is unnecessary if the steamer basket has very fine holes.) Spread the rice evenly over the cheesecloth. Place the container over rapidly boiling water; do not let the rice come in contact with the water. Cover tightly and steam until the rice is tender, about 25 minutes for white rice, or 1 hour for brown or black rice. Add boiling water to the steamer if necessary to maintain level when cooking brown or black rice. Remove and serve, or use as directed in recipes.

Makes about 3 cups white rice, or 3 to 4 cups brown or black rice; serves 4.

VARIATION: For stickier rice, place the drained soaked rice in a pot with 1½ cups water or coconut milk (page 16), bring to boil over high heat, cover, reduce heat to very low, and cook for 15 minutes. When cooking more than 1 cup of rice, add only 1 cup of water for each additional cup of rice. Remove from heat and let stand, covered, for 15 minutes. Transfer the rice to a cheesecloth-lined steamer as described above and steam over boiling water until tender, about 15 minutes for white rice, or 45 minutes for brown or black rice.

Basic Wild Rice

Any vegetable or meat stock can also be used as the cooking liquid. If you like a chewy texture, reduce the cooking time; for softer rice, increase the cooking time. Once the grains pop open as directed in many recipes the rice is overcooked for my taste.

Place the rice in a wire strainer and wash thoroughly under running cold water until the water runs clear. Drain.

In a saucepan, bring the liquid to a boil over high heat. Add the rice and salt to taste and return to a boil. Stir once, cover, reduce the heat to low, and simmer until just tender, about 35 to 40 minutes. Remove from the heat and drain off any excess water. Cover the pot with a piece of paper toweling, replace the lid, and let stand until the rice is dry, about 5 minutes. Add the butter, if desired, and fluff with a fork, lifting from the bottom instead of stirring.

Alternatively, combine the rinsed rice, cooking liquid, and salt in a baking dish. Cover tightly and place in a preheated 350° F oven until done, about 1½ hours, adding a little water if needed during the last 30 minutes. Or combine the ingredients in a microwave baking dish, stir, cover, and cook at full power for 5 minutes. Reduce the power to 50 percent and cook for 30 minutes longer. Let stand for 15 minutes, then drain off excess liquid. Rid the rice of any dampness by using paper toweling as described in the stove-top method. Whether rice has been baked or microwaved, add the butter, if desired, and fluff with a fork.

Makes 3½ to 4 cups; serves 4 to 6.

1 cup wild rice
3 cups homemade chicken or beef stock, canned broth, or water
Salt
1 tablespoon unsalted butter (optional)

Storing Raw Rice

Upon opening any sealed package of rice or purchasing the grain in bulk, place the unused portion in an airtight container and store in a cool place. White polished rice and wild rice keep indefinitely, while brown rice has a shelf life of only 6 months due to the oil in the bran covering. Refrigeration of brown rice will prolong its storage life by several months.

Storing and Reheating Cooked Rice

I enjoy keeping a container of cooked rice on hand for last-minute fried rice or other quick meals, so I nearly always cook extra. To store, let hot rice stand until completely cold, then cover with foil or plastic wrap or transfer to a container with a tight-fitting lid. The rice will steam and become soggy if covered while still warm. It keeps well refrigerated for up to 10 days, or can be frozen for about 3 months.

To reheat, transfer the rice to a baking dish, add 2 tablespoons hot water or the original cooking liquid per cup of rice, cover tightly with foil and place in a preheated 325° F oven until hot, about 30 minutes. Remove cover, add a little butter if desired, fluff with a fork, and serve.

Alternatively, place the rice in a saucepan, add 2 tablespoons of hot liquid per cup of rice, cover, and place over low heat until hot, about 5 minutes; stir and fluff occasionally with a fork.

To reheat rice in a microwave, place it in a microwave container, add 2 tablespoons of hot liquid per cup of rice, cover, and microwave at 50 percent power until hot, about 2 minutes.

SAVORY DISHES

Greek Stuffed Grape Leaves (*Dolmas*)

Versions of this well-known appetizer are served in Greece and throughout the Middle East. Well covered, *dolmas* will keep for a week or longer in the refrigerator; bring to room temperature and refresh with a squeeze of lemon before serving.

Wash and drain the rice as described on page 12.

Heat 3 tablespoons of the olive oil in a sauté pan or skillet over medium-high heat. Add the yellow onion and sauté until soft but not brown, about 5 minutes. Transfer to a mixing bowl and add the drained rice, ½ cup of the remaining olive oil, green onions, parsley, mint, pine nuts, cinnamon, allspice, salt, and pepper. Set aside.

Rinse the grape leaves under running cold water to remove as much brine as possible, pat dry, and stack on a plate. Place 1 leaf at a time, shiny side down, on a flat work surface. Cut off and discard the tough stem end. Spoon about 1 tablespoon of the rice mixture in the center near the base of the leaf. Fold the stem end over to cover the filling; fold both sides inward lengthwise and then tightly roll leaf toward pointed tip end to form a compact packet. Repeat with the remaining leaves and filling.

Pour about 2 tablespoons of the remaining olive oil in the bottom of a large pot and strew with a layer of parsley stems to prevent grape leaves from sticking. Arrange the stuffed leaves, seam side down and almost touching, on top of the parsley, making as many layers as necessary. Drizzle the remaining 6 tablespoons olive oil, the lemon juice, and ½ cup stock, broth, or water over the leaves. Top with a heat-resistant plate and weight with a heavy can to keep leaves from unwinding during cooking. Cover the pot, bring to a gentle boil, reduce the heat to low, and cook until rice is tender, about 1 hour. During cooking, add a little heated liquid as needed to keep *dolmas* moist. Remove from the heat and cool in the pot.

Sprinkle with lemon juice to taste, garnish with lemon zest, and serve at room temperature.

Makes about 50 *dolmas*; serves 20 as a starter.

1 cup long-grain white rice
1 cup plus 3 tablespoons olive oil
1 cup finely chopped yellow onion
3 green onions, including green tops, finely chopped
¼ cup minced fresh parsley
2 tablespoons minced fresh mint
½ cup pine nuts
1 teaspoon ground cinnamon
½ teaspoon ground allspice
½ teaspoon salt
¼ teaspoon freshly ground black pepper
1 jar (16 ounces) grape leaves packed in brine
Several stems of fresh parsley
About ¾ cup freshly squeezed lemon juice
About 1 cup homemade chicken stock, canned chicken broth, or water, heated
Additional freshly squeezed lemon juice
Grated or minced lemon zest for garnish

Japanese Seasoned Rice with Scattered Toppings (*Chirashi-Zushi*)

You probably won't encounter this authentic Japanese sushi preparation in most American sushi bars. Vary toppings according to taste and availability; most ingredients can be found in Japanese markets and many supermarkets.

Cook the rice in water according to directions on page 15, omitting butter and onion.

Just before the rice is ready, combine the vinegar, sugar, and salt in a small saucepan and stir over high heat until the sugar is dissolved, about 2 minutes. Cool briefly.

Fluff the warm rice with the tines of a fork and transfer it to a wide shallow wooden or ceramic bowl or wooden tray; do not use a metal container. Pouring in a little at a time, add the vinegar mixture to the rice, turning the rice carefully with a wooden spatula to avoid breaking the kernels. To make the rice glossy, turn the rice continuously while fanning with a paper or straw fan or a hair dryer set on cool until the rice is cool and all the liquid is absorbed, about 10 minutes. Cover and store at room temperature for up to several hours; do not refrigerate.

To prepare the toppings, soak the seaweed in the soy sauce and enough warm water to cover until soft, about 30 minutes. Drain, rinse in cold water, and drain again, pressing out all liquid.

Slice the asparagus, green beans, or edible pod peas on the diagonal into 1-inch lengths. Steam or cook in boiling water just until crisp-tender, then quickly chill in ice water to stop cooking and preserve color. Drain well and reserve.

To serve, spoon the rice out onto a large platter or distribute evenly on individual plates. Scatter the seaweed, cooked vegetables, bamboo shoots, ginger, sesame seeds and shrimp, if using, over the top.

Serves 8 as a starter or part of a Japanese meal.

SUSHI RICE
2 cups short-grain white rice
¼ cup rice vinegar
3 tablespoons granulated sugar
1 teaspoon salt

TOPPINGS
¼ cup dried *hijiki* seaweed
2 tablespoons soy sauce, preferably *tamari*
6 ounces fresh asparagus, green beans, or edible pod peas
1 or 2 whole canned bamboo shoots, thinly sliced, or 1 can (6½ ounces) sliced bamboo shoots, drained and sliced into thin julienne
Sliced pickled red ginger (*benishoga*)
Black sesame seeds, lightly toasted
12 small shrimp, cooked and peeled (optional)

Chinese Sizzling Rice Soup

1 cup short-grain white rice
1½ quarts homemade chicken stock
    or canned chicken broth
3 green onions, including most of
    the green tops, minced
Soy sauce
Asian-style sesame oil
Hot chili oil
2 cups peanut oil or other vegetable
    oil for deep frying

Chunks of crusty rice are deep fried, then quickly added to this simple soup at the table to create a sizzling explosion. Traditionally made from the crisp layer of kernels that sticks to the bottom of the pot when cooking rice, here's an easier way to prepare the crusts. You'll need to start this recipe the day before you plan to serve the soup.

Cook the rice in water as described on page 15, omitting butter and onion.

Preheat the oven to 250° F.

Press the cooked rice into a shallow pan, such as a 9-by-13-inch glass baking dish, to create a thick, even layer. Transfer to the oven and heat until the rice is completely dried out, about 30 minutes. Remove from oven and use immediately or let stand, loosely covered, for up to several hours at room temperature.

In a saucepan, bring the stock or broth to a boil over medium-high heat. Reduce the heat to low and add the green onions and soy sauce, sesame oil, and chili oil to taste. Simmer 5 minutes, then keep warm.

Just before serving, heat the peanut oil in a wok or skillet to 360° F, or until a small piece of bread dropped into the oil turns golden within a few seconds. Break off pieces of the rice crust and fry a few at a time, turning several times, until golden brown, about 5 minutes. Drain briefly on paper toweling. Pour the soup into a preheated tureen or serving bowl, place the hot fried rice crusts on a plate, and immediately carry the soup and crusts to the table. Carefully slide the crusts into the soup, then ladle into individual bowls.

Serves 4 as a soup course.

Canadian Wild Rice and Wild Mushroom Soup

Two earthy flavors combine in this creamy soup. Soaked dried mushrooms can be substituted when fresh ones are unavailable.

Wash and drain the rice as described on page 19.

In a large saucepan, combine the rice and the stock or broth and bring to a boil over high heat. Reduce the heat to low, cover, and simmer until the rice is very soft, about 1½ hours. Drain the rice in a wire sieve placed over a saucepan (off the heat) to catch the stock. Transfer the rice to a food processor or blender, add about 1 cup of the reserved stock, and purée until smooth. With the back of a wooden spoon, rub as much of the puréed rice as possible through a sieve into the remaining stock, discarding any rice that won't go through the sieve. Set aside.

Remove and discard any tough stems from the mushrooms. Finely chop the mushrooms in a food processor or by hand.

Melt 2 tablespoons of the butter in a sauté pan or skillet over medium heat. Add the shallot and sauté until soft, about 3 minutes. Add the chopped mushrooms and lemon juice and sauté until the liquid has evaporated, about 5 minutes longer. Add the shallot-mushroom mixture to the rice mixture and place over medium heat. Add the cream and thyme. Bring to a boil, stirring frequently, then reduce the heat to low and simmer, uncovered, until thick and creamy, about 15 minutes. Season to taste with salt, pepper, and sherry or lemon juice.

To serve, ladle the soup into bowls and garnish with thyme sprigs.

Serves 6 as a soup course.

1 cup wild rice
2 quarts homemade beef, chicken, or vegetable stock, or canned broth
1 pound fresh wild mushrooms— *chanterelles*, morels, *porcini*, or *shiitake*
3 tablespoons unsalted butter
3 tablespoons minced shallot
2 tablespoons freshly squeezed lemon juice
2 cups heavy (whipping) cream
1 tablespoon minced fresh thyme, or 1 teaspoon dried thyme, crumbled
Salt
Freshly ground black pepper
Dry sherry or freshly squeezed lemon juice
Fresh thyme sprigs for garnish

Italian Creamy Rice with Saffron (*Risotto alla Milanese*)

1½ cups short-grain white rice,
  preferably arborio or pearl
About 5 cups homemade chicken
  stock or canned chicken broth
½ teaspoon powdered saffron, or
  1 teaspoon crushed saffron
  threads, more or less to taste
¼ pound (1 stick) unsalted butter
½ cup minced shallot or yellow onion
1 garlic clove, minced or pressed
½ dry white wine
½ pound fresh tender asparagus, cut
  into 1-inch lengths, cooked until
  crisp-tender, quickly chilled in
  icewater, and drained
1 cup freshly grated Parmesan cheese,
  preferably Parmigiano-Reggiano
Salt
Freshly ground black pepper
Freshly grated Parmesan cheese
  for passing

Risotto is rice that has a creamy consistency and a firm bite. To achieve this result calls for a cooking method that combines almost continuous stirring with the gradual addition of small amounts of hot stock. Use this technique, with or without saffron, to make *risotto* with almost anything you can dream up. In place of the asparagus, use sautéed cultivated or wild mushrooms, or other vegetables, or cooked chicken, shellfish, or meats.

Wash and drain the rice as described on page 12.

In a saucepan, bring the stock or broth to a boil over high heat, then reduce the heat to low and keep the broth at a simmer during the rest of the cooking time. Remove ½ cup of the stock and stir the saffron into it; reserve.

Heat 7 tablespoons of the butter in a heavy, deep sauté pan or skillet over medium-high heat. Add the shallot or onion and sauté until lightly golden. Add the garlic and drained rice and sauté until all the grains of the rice are well coated, about 2 minutes. Stir in the white wine and cook, stirring, until the wine has evaporated, about 3 minutes. Add ½ cup of the simmering broth, adjusting heat if the liquid is evaporating too quickly. Keep liquid and rice simmering and stir almost continuously, scraping the bottom and sides of the pan, until the liquid has been absorbed.

Add hot broth ½ cup at a time each time the rice becomes dry, continuing to stir. Use the saffron-flavored broth after the first 15 minutes of cooking. As the risotto approaches completion, add the broth only ¼ cup at a time. You may not need all the broth before the rice is done, or you may need more liquid, in which case add hot water. Cook until the rice is tender but firm to the bite, about 25 minutes total. When properly cooked, the rice should be creamy but not soupy.

A couple of minutes before you think the rice will be done, stir in the asparagus, the cheese, and the remaining 1 tablespoon butter. Add salt and pepper to taste. Serve immediately. Pass additional Parmesan at the table.

Serves 4 to 6 as a first course or side dish.

Rice and Peas, Italian Style
(Risi e Bisi)

1 cup short-grain white rice,
    preferably arborio or pearl
4 tablespoons unsalted butter
3 tablespoons minced yellow onion
2½ cups homemade chicken stock
    or canned chicken broth
½ cup dry white wine
2 pounds fresh green peas, shelled,
    or 1½ cups frozen petite green
    peas, thawed
4 ounces prosciutto or flavorful
    baked ham, thinly sliced and cut
    into julienne (optional)
½ cup freshly grated Parmesan
    cheese, preferably
    Parmigiano-Reggiano
Salt
Freshly ground black pepper
Freshly grated Parmesan cheese
    for passing

Some Italian cooks prefer this dish quite moist and served in a bowl with a soup spoon; if you wish to follow suit, add a little extra stock. Either way the classic combination makes a great beginning or light main course.

Wash and drain the rice as described on page 12.

Melt the butter in a saucepan, add onion, and sauté over medium heat until soft but not golden. Stir in the rice and sauté until all the grains are well coated with butter, about 2 minutes. Add the stock or broth and wine and bring to a boil. Cover, reduce the heat to low, and simmer, stirring occasionally, until the rice is tender but firm to the bite and most of the liquid has been absorbed, about 20 minutes.

While the rice is cooking, cook the peas in a small amount of water just until they are tender, about 10 minutes for fresh peas, or 5 minutes for thawed.

When the rice is cooked, stir in the peas, ham, if using, cheese, and salt and pepper to taste. Serve immediately. Pass additional Parmesan at the table.

Serves 4 as a first course, or 2 as a main course.

Rice and Cheese Molds

2 cups long-grain white rice
1 small to medium-sized eggplant,
    cut crosswise into 6½-inch-thick
    slices
About ¼ cup olive oil, preferably
    extra-virgin
Salt
Freshly ground black pepper
4 quarts water
4 tablespoons unsalted butter
½ sweet red pepper, membrane and
    seeds discarded, minced
2 teaspoons minced fresh thyme,
    or 1 teaspoon dried thyme,
    crumbled
1 cup freshly grated Parmesan cheese,
    preferably Parmigiano-Reggiano
Freshly ground white pepper
Unsalted butter, softened,
    for greasing
½ sweet red pepper, membrane and
    seeds discarded, cut lengthwise
    into thin julienne
4 ounces Italian Fontina cheese,
    thinly sliced
Fresh thyme sprigs or other fresh
    herb leaves for garnish

Rice baked in a mold looks and tastes great preceding or alongside grilled fish, poultry, or meats. Ramekins, custard cups, or metal timbales may be used for individual servings. Select an eggplant a bit larger in diameter than your individual baking dishes. Or layer the ingredients in a round 6- to 8-cup mold or baking dish, and top with a layer of overlapping eggplant slices. Cut into wedges to serve.

Wash and drain the rice as directed on page 12. Preheat the oven to 400° F.

Brush the eggplant slices with olive oil, season to taste with salt and pepper, arrange in a baking dish, and bake until tender, about 30 minutes. Reserve.

In a stockpot, bring the water to a boil over high heat. Add about 1 tablespoon salt and the drained rice, stirring vigorously a few times. Return to a boil and cook, uncovered, until the rice is *al dente*, about 12 minutes. Drain in a colander, then transfer to a mixing bowl.

Heat the butter in a small pan over medium-high heat, add the minced sweet pepper, and sauté until the pepper is soft, about 5 minutes. Stir in the thyme and cook 1 minute. Add pepper mixture to the rice. Stir in the Parmesan cheese and salt and white pepper to taste.

Generously butter the bottom and sides of 6 individual 1-cup molds or baking dishes. Add the sweet pepper strips to create a pattern on the bottom of each container (which will become the top of each serving). Evenly distribute about one-third of the rice mixture among the 6 molds, pressing gently to eliminate air pockets; top with thin layers of the Fontina. Continue layering until all ingredients are used up, ending with rice. Top each mold with an eggplant slice, again pressing gently. Bake until the cheese melts and the flavors are well blended, about 15 minutes. Remove from the oven and let stand for about 5 minutes.

To unmold, slide a knife around the inside edge of each mold and invert onto individual plates. Garnish with herb sprig and serve warm.

Serves 6 as a first course or side dish.

Green Rice Salad

Fresh herbs are the secret to this glorious salad that was first served to me by San Francisco garden master Stephen Marcus. Use herbs in whatever combination you find appealing. Accompanied by hot cornbread or other home-baked bread, the hearty salad is a whole meal. It is equally delicious as a salad course, buffet dish, or accompaniment to grilled or roasted chicken, fish, or meat.

To make the vinaigrette, combine the oil, vinegar, lemon juice, green onions, parsley, garlic, sugar, and salt and pepper to taste. Whisk to blend well and reserve.

Cook the brown rice in water as directed on page 15, omitting the butter and onion. Fluff with a fork, transfer to a large mixing bowl, and cool slightly. Gently toss the warm rice with about one-third of the vinaigrette. Fluff the rice frequently until it cools completely, then cover and let stand at room temperature for several hours or as long as overnight.

Cook the white rice in water as directed on page 15, omitting the onion and butter. Fluff with a fork and cool to room temperature, then add it to the marinated brown rice in a large bowl. Toss with the green onions, minced herbs, cheese, green peas, and remaining vinaigrette to taste. Let stand for about 30 minutes for flavors to blend.

Place the pine nuts in a small, heavy skillet over medium heat and toast, shaking the pan or stirring frequently, until lightly golden, about 5 minutes. Pour onto a plate to cool.

To serve, mound the rice salad on a bed of shredded lettuce. Garnish with the toasted pine nuts, herb sprigs, and flowers.

Serves 12 to 14 as a salad course, or 6 to 8 as a main course.

BALSAMIC VINAIGRETTE
2 cups olive oil, preferably
    extra-virgin
½ cup balsamic vinegar
¼ cup freshly squeezed lemon juice
6 to 8 green onions, including
    green tops, minced
½ cup chopped fresh parsley
1 teaspoon minced or pressed garlic
2 teaspoons granulated sugar
Salt
Freshly ground black pepper

2 cups long-grain brown rice
2 cups long-grain white rice
6 green onions, including green tops,
    finely chopped
2 to 3 cups minced mixed fresh
    herbs—basil, cilantro (coriander),
    mint, parsley, tarragon, and/or
    watercress
1 cup shredded white Cheddar cheese
2 cups cooked fresh green peas or
    thawed frozen petite peas
¼ cup pine nuts
Shredded lettuce
Sprigs of same fresh herbs as above
    for garnish
Pesticide-free, nontoxic flowers such
    as wild mustard and
    forget-me-nots (optional)

Spicy Rice and Shrimp Salad

Fiery hot and refreshingly cool seasonings unique to the cooking of Southeast Asia give this salad a special exotic flair. When available, steamed fiddlehead fern sprouts make an interesting garnish.

To make the vinaigrette, combine the vinegar, fish or soy sauce, oils, and lime juice. Whisk to blend well and reserve.

Cook the rice in water as directed on page 15, omitting butter and onion. Fluff with a fork, transfer to a large mixing bowl, and cool slightly. Gently toss the warm rice with about one-third of the dressing. Fluff frequently until the rice cools completely.

Add the green onions, carrots, sweet pepper, chili pepper, mint, cilantro, and most of the shrimp, reserving some for garnish. Toss with remaining dressing for taste. Mound on a serving platter, sprinkle with peanuts, surround with bean sprouts, if using, and garnish with the cilantro sprigs, lime wedges, and reserved shrimp.

Serves 6 to 8 as a salad course, or 4 as a main course.

SESAME-CHILI DRESSING
½ cup rice vinegar
½ cup fish sauce or soy sauce
¼ cup Asian-style sesame oil
¼ cup hot chili oil, or to taste
¼ cup freshly squeezed lime juice

2 cups long-grain white rice
6 green onions, including green tops, sliced
2 carrots, peeled and diced
1 sweet red pepper, membrane and seeds discarded, diced
1 to 2 teaspoons minced fresh chili pepper, or to taste
½ cup chopped fresh mint
¼ cup chopped fresh cilantro (coriander)
1 pound medium-sized shrimp, cooked, shelled, and deveined
⅓ cup chopped unsalted peanuts
About 2 cups fresh bean sprouts (optional)
Fresh cilantro sprigs for garnish
Lime wedges for garnish

Middle Eastern Pilaf

½ cup wild rice
4¼ cups homemade chicken stock or
   canned chicken broth
½ cup long-grain white rice
½ cup long-grain brown Wehani rice
½ cup long-grain brown rice
12 tablespoons (¾ cup or 1½ sticks)
   unsalted butter
6 tablespoons finely chopped
   yellow onion
1 cup pine nuts or slivered blanched
   almonds
1 cup dried currants, plumped in hot
   water to cover and drained
¾ cup chopped fresh mint
Whole fresh mint leaves for garnish

For this festive party dish, cook several types of rice separately, then toss them together with almonds and mint. A simple everyday pilaf can be made using just one type of rice. Follow this basic method to create your own pilaf dishes: add other cooked grains such as millet, buckwheat groats, or wheat or rye berries; bits of cooked lamb, pork, or poultry; chopped green onions, sweet pepper, or carrots; and/or nuts such as cashews, pistachios, or peanuts.

Cook the wild rice in 1½ cups of the stock or broth as directed on page 19. Wash and drain each of the other rices as described on page 12, keeping them separate.

In three separate saucepans, heat 2 tablespoons butter over medium-high heat, add 2 tablespoons of the onion to each pan, and sauté until soft, about 5 minutes. Add one of the drained rices to each pan and sauté until every grain is well coated with butter, about 2 minutes. Add ¾ cup stock or broth to the white rice and 1 cup stock or broth to each brown rice. Bring to a boil, then stir once, reduce the heat to low, cover tightly, and simmer the white rice for 17 minutes and each of the brown rices for 45 minutes.

Melt 3 tablespoons of the remaining butter in a small skillet over medium heat, add the pine nuts or almonds, and cook, stirring constantly, until golden brown. Remove to paper toweling to drain.

Preheat the oven to 350° F.

In a large bowl, combine all of the cooked rices, fluffing with a fork to mix the different types thoroughly and to separate grains. Stir in the butter-toasted nuts, drained currants, and the chopped mint. Melt the remaining 3 tablespoons butter and stir into the rice mixture. Transfer the pilaf to a well-greased 8-cup ring mold, cover with foil, and heat in the oven for 20 minutes. Invert onto a plate and garnish with the whole mint leaves. Alternatively, heat and serve the pilaf in an attractive baking dish.

Serves 8 to 12 as a side dish.

Four Mexican Rice Dishes

The daily rice of most Mexican households is red, similar to the type associated with Mexican restaurants north of the border, while zesty herb-laced green rice is served for holiday or other special meals. White rice is reserved for weddings and christenings, but instead of being plain, it's subtly infused with cilantro and jalapeños. Yellow rice is a tradition of the Yucatán, where achiote, the tiny bright red seeds of the annatto tree, are used to color the grain a cheery yellow. Look for these seeds in Latin American markets; they are also sold in paste and extract forms. For a Mexican party, you might want to prepare all four versions.

To make red rice, wash and drain the rice as described on page 12.

Heat the oil in a saucepan over medium heat. Add the drained rice, onion, and sweet pepper and cook, stirring frequently, until all the ingredients are lightly golden, about 8 minutes. Add the garlic and cook 1 minute longer. Stir in the tomato purée and chili pepper, if using, and cook 1 minute longer. Add the stock or broth and salt to taste. Bring to a boil, stir once, reduce heat to low, cover tightly, and simmer for 20 minutes. Remove pan from heat and let stand, covered, 5 minutes. With a fork, mix in the peas and carrots, if using, garnish with the red pepper strips, and serve.

Serves 4 to 6 as a side dish.

RED RICE (*Arroz a la Mexicana*)
1 cup long-grain white rice
2 tablespoons vegetable oil
½ cup finely chopped yellow onion
¼ cup finely chopped red sweet pepper
2 garlic cloves, minced or pressed
2 medium-sized ripe tomatoes, peeled and puréed in food processor or blender, or 1 can (15 ounces) tomatoes, drained and puréed
1 fresh red chili pepper, membrane and seeds discarded, minced (optional)
1½ cups homemade chicken stock or canned chicken broth
Salt
¼ cup shelled fresh green peas, or thawed frozen petite green peas, cooked crisp-tender and drained (optional)
1 large carrot, peeled, cut into small dice, cooked crisp-tender, and drained (optional)
Red sweet pepper strips for garnish

GREEN RICE *(Arroz Verde)*

1 cup long-grain white rice
2 fresh poblano chili peppers,
    membrane and seeds discarded,
    coarsely chopped
½ green sweet pepper, membrane
    and seeds discarded, coarsely
    chopped
3 garlic cloves
½ cup coarsely chopped fresh
    cilantro (coriander)
½ cup coarsely chopped fresh parsley,
    preferably flat-leaf type
¼ cup safflower or other
    good-quality vegetable oil
½ cup finely chopped yellow onion
1⅓ cups homemade chicken stock,
    canned chicken broth, or water
Salt
Fresh cilantro leaves for garnish
Fresh parsley leaves for garnish

To make green rice, wash and drain the rice as described on page 12.

Combine the chilies, sweet pepper, garlic, cilantro, and parsley in a food processor or blender and purée. Reserve.

Heat the oil in a saucepan over medium heat. Add the onion and sauté until soft but not browned, about 5 minutes. Stir in the drained rice and sauté until all the grains are well coated with oil, about 2 minutes longer. Add the puréed chili mixture and cook about 2 minutes longer. Add the stock, broth, or water and salt to taste. Bring to a boil, stir once, reduce the heat to low, cover tightly, and simmer for 17 minutes. Remove pan from heat and let stand, covered, 5 minutes. Fluff with a fork, garnish with the cilantro and parsley, and serve.

Serves 4 to 6 as a side dish.

To make white rice, wash and drain the rice as described on page 12.

Heat the oil in a saucepan over medium heat. Add the onion and sauté until soft but not browned, about 5 minutes. Stir in the drained rice and sauté until all the grains are well coated with oil, about 2 minutes longer. Stir in the garlic and sauté 1 minute longer. Add the stock, broth, or water and salt to taste and bring to a boil. Stir once, lay the cilantro and chili peppers on top, reduce the heat to low, cover tightly, and simmer for 17 minutes. Remove pan from the heat and let stand, covered, for 5 minutes. Remove and discard the cilantro sprigs; remove the chili peppers and reserve them to use as a garnish, if desired. Fluff the rice with a fork, garnish with the cooked chili peppers and fresh cilantro or parsley leaves, and serve.

Serves 4 to 6 as a side dish.

To make yellow rice, wash and drain the rice as described on page 12.

Heat the oil in a saucepan over low heat. Add the seeds, cook until the seeds turn dark brown, remove with a slotted spoon, and discard.

Increase the heat under the orange-colored oil to medium-high, add the onion and the drained rice, and sauté until both are golden, about 8 minutes. Stir in the garlic and sauté 1 minute longer. Add the stock, broth, or water and salt to taste. Bring to a boil, stir once, reduce the heat to low, cover tightly, and simmer for 17 minutes. Remove from the heat and let stand, covered, for 5 minutes. Fluff with a fork, garnish with chervil or parsley, and serve.

Serves 4 to 6 as a side dish.

WHITE RICE (Arroz Blanco)
1 cup long-grain white rice
¼ cup vegetable oil
⅓ cup finely chopped yellow onion
3 garlic cloves, minced or pressed
1½ cups homemade chicken stock,
    canned chicken broth, or water
Salt
Several long sprigs fresh cilantro
    (coriander)
2 or 3 whole fresh or canned jalapeño
    chili peppers
Fresh cilantro or parsley leaves,
    preferably flat-leaf type, for
    garnish

YELLOW RICE (Arroz Gualdo)
1 cup long-grain white rice
3 tablespoons vegetable oil
1½ tablespoons *achiote* seeds (annatto
    seeds)
½ cup finely chopped yellow onion
1 garlic clove, minced or pressed
1½ cups homemade chicken stock,
    canned chicken broth, or water
Salt
Fresh chervil or parsley sprigs,
    preferably flat-leaf type, for
    garnish

Indonesian Rice Packets (*Lontong*)

2 cups short- or medium-grain
  white rice
Peel of 1 lime, removed in 1 piece
3 cups coconut milk (page 16;
  optional)
3 cups water, or 6 cups water if not
  using coconut milk
6 pieces fresh or thawed frozen
  banana leaves, cut into 12-inch
  squares, or 6 pieces foil, cut the
  same dimension

Wrapping rice tightly in a package for cooking causes the expanding kernels to form a solid mass that is easily sliced and then eaten with the fingers. This unique rice preparation complements spicy Asian dishes and is perfect picnic fare. Though *lontong* is traditionally made with unseasoned rice, the hint of lime and coconut appeals to Western palates. Look for fresh banana leaves in florist shops, or fresh or frozen ones in markets that cater to Southeast Asians.

Wash and drain the rice as described on page 12.

In a saucepan, combine the drained rice, lime peel, coconut milk, if using, and water and bring to a boil over medium-high heat. Stir once, reduce the heat to low, cover tightly, and simmer for 15 minutes. Remove from the heat and let stand, covered, until cool, up to 30 minutes. Discard lime peel.

If using fresh banana leaves, place the pieces in a bowl, cover with boiling water, and let stand to soften, about 5 minutes; drain. Lay the leaves or foil squares on a flat surface. Scoop an equal portion of the rice onto each piece. Pat the rice to form a sausage shape about 2 inches in diameter and 6 inches long that runs parallel with the veins of the leaf. Roll the leaf around the rice, maintaining the sausage shape, then pinch each end together and fold it back over the cylinder. Tie the packets in several places with narrow strips of softened banana leaf or cotton string. If using foil, roll it around the rice, then twist each end together; do not tie.

Place the packets on a steamer rack and steam for 1 hour over water that remains at a rolling boil; add water as necessary to maintain level. Alternatively, immerse the packets in a pot of boiling water and boil for 45 minutes, adding additional boiling water as needed to keep packets covered. Remove packets from the steamer or boiling water and cool to room temperature, then chill for 6 hours.

Serve cold or bring to room temperature. Unwrap and cut into ½-inch-thick slices.

Serves 6 as an accompaniment.

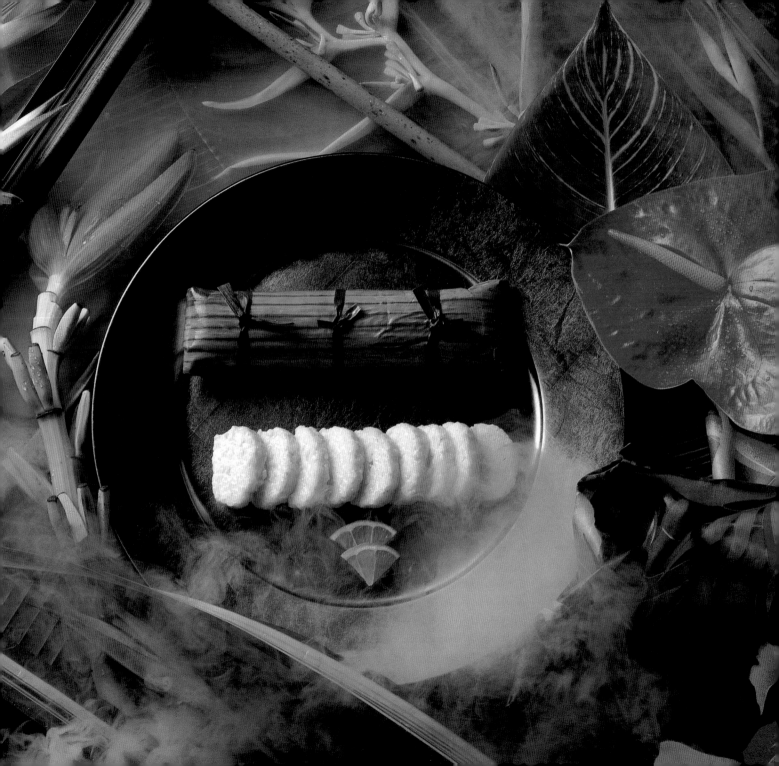

Rice Stuffings or Dressings

My naturalized sister and kitchen assistant, Gail High, shares her favorite rice dish here. Though it is called a "stuffing" for a roast chicken, Gail usually bakes it in a separate pan and serves it as a side dish. Likewise, I prefer my southern-style turkey stuffing baked alongside. Of course, both of these mixtures are also great when cooked inside a bird.

To make chicken or duck stuffing, place the warm rice in a mixing bowl. Stir in currants, almonds, onion, butter, basil, parsley, egg, if using, and salt and pepper to taste. Mix thoroughly. Use to stuff a chicken or duck for roasting or spoon into a baking dish, cover tightly with foil, and place in a preheated 350° F oven until heated through, about 30 minutes. Alternatively, heat in a microwave oven for about 5 minutes.

Enough to stuff 1 5- to 7-pound bird, or serves 6 as a side dish.

To make turkey stuffing, melt the butter in a sauté pan or large, heavy skillet, over medium-high heat. Add the sausage, onion, celery, and sweet pepper and cook until the sausage is done and the vegetables are soft, about 5 minutes. Stir in the garlic and sauté 1 minute. Remove from heat and stir in the parsley, giblets and neck meat, rice, wild rice, oysters, pecans, and Worcestershire sauce. Mix thoroughly and season to taste with salt and pepper.

Use to stuff a turkey for roasting or spoon into a baking dish, cover tightly with foil, and place in a preheated 350° F oven until heated through, about 30 minutes. Alternatively, heat in a microwave oven for about 5 minutes.

Enough to stuff a 18- to 20 pound turkey, or serves 8 to 10 as a side dish.

CHICKEN OR DUCK STUFFING
2 cups warm cooked rice (page 15)
½ cup dried currants, plumped in hot water to cover and drained
1 cup blanched almonds, finely chopped
½ cup finely chopped yellow onion
4 tablespoons unsalted butter, melted
⅓ cup minced fresh basil
½ cup minced fresh parsley
1 egg (if using as a stuffing)
Salt
Freshly ground black pepper

TURKEY STUFFING
4 tablespoons unsalted butter
½ pound mild or hot sausage, casing discarded and meat crumbled
2 cups finely chopped yellow onion
2 cups finely chopped celery
1 cup finely chopped red sweet pepper, membrane and seeds discarded
1 entire garlic head, minced or pressed
½ cup minced fresh parsley, preferably flat-leaf type
Cooked turkey giblets and meat from neck, chopped
2 cups warm cooked rice (page 15)
1 cup cooked wild rice (page 19)
1 pint small whole oysters or chopped large oysters, drained (optional)
1 cup chopped pecans
2 tablespoons Worcestershire sauce
Salt
Freshly ground black pepper

Persian Dilled Rice
with Lima Beans *(Polo)*

The Iranians are true rice connoisseurs, devoting much time and attention to its preparation. When cooked plain by the following method, rice is termed *chilau, chelou,* or *chelo.* When other ingredients are added to the rice it becomes a *polo,* the Persian equivalent of Indian *pilau* or Turkish *pilav.*

This presentation is a delicious example of the centuries-old tradition of teaming rice with beans that's practiced in cuisines around the globe. For variety, stir cooked fowl, beef, or lamb into the rice before steaming.

Wash and drain the rice as described on page 12.

In a large bowl, combine the rice with enough cold water to cover by 1 inch. Stir in the salt and let stand overnight. Drain the water into a large pot. Add 3 quarts cold water and the rice. Bring to a boil over high heat and boil 1 minute; drain immediately.

In a large, heavy pot, heat enough of the butter to cover the bottom of the pan. Spread about 1 cup of the rice in the bottom of the pan. Transfer the rest of the rice to a mixing bowl and toss it with the cooked lima beans, chopped dill, and salt to taste. Spoon the mixture on top of the rice in the pan, shaping it into a cone. Make a slight indention in the top of the rice and pour the remaining butter over. Cover the pot with a clean cloth towel to catch and hold the steam as it rises, then cover with a lid and fold the corners of the towel up on top of the lid. Place the pot over medium-low heat for 15 minutes, then reduce the heat to very low and cook until the rice is tender, about 35 minutes. Transfer the pan to a cold surface and let stand for about 5 minutes.

To serve, spoon the rice onto a large platter, then scrape out pieces of the golden, crisp crust (known as *dig*) from the bottom of the pot. Garnish the rice with the crisp crust, chopped dill, and dill sprigs.

Serves 8 as a side dish.

2 cups long-grain rice, preferably basmati
About 4 quarts water
1 tablespoon salt
½ pound (2 sticks) unsalted butter, melted
1½ cups shelled fresh small lima beans, or 1 package (10 ounces) thawed frozen lima beans, cooked crisp-tender
½ cup chopped fresh dill, or ¼ cup dried dill weed, crumbled
Salt
Chopped fresh dill for garnish
Fresh dill sprigs for garnish

Creole Beans and Rice

1½ pounds dried red (kidney) beans
or white (navy) beans

1 pound flavorful baked ham, diced
into 1-inch cubes

1 pound andouille or other smoked
pork sausage, sliced into ¾-inch
lengths

2 cups finely chopped yellow onion

1½ cups finely chopped celery

1 cup finely chopped green sweet
pepper, membrane and seeds
discarded

4 green onions, including green tops,
sliced

1 tablespoon minced or pressed garlic

¼ cup minced fresh parsley,
preferably flat-leaf type

3 bay leaves

2 tablespoons minced fresh thyme,
or 2 teaspoons dried thyme,
crumbled

1 tablespoon minced fresh oregano,
or 1 teaspoon dried oregano,
crumbled

Salt

Freshly ground black pepper

Ground cayenne pepper

Tabasco sauce

2 cups long-grain rice

Minced fresh parsley or green onions
for garnish

Every Monday in New Orleans, as has been the custom for over two centuries, vast pots of creamy beans are ladled over rice, a carryover from the old washday lunch when beans slowly simmered while the laundry took about as long to dry in the Louisiana humidity. Most people think this classic is only prepared with red beans, but New Orleans cooks work the same wonders with white beans.

New Orleanians prefer their beans over plain white rice, but I find the nutty taste of brown rice or the onion-flavored Perfect Rice on page 15 more satisfying. Since beans and rice combine to form a complete protein, I eliminate the meat when cooking this dish for vegetarian friends.

Rinse the beans well, then place in a bowl and add enough cold water to cover. Soak overnight at room temperature.

Combine the ham and sausage in a cast-iron dutch oven or other large, heavy pot over medium-high heat. Sauté until fat is rendered, about 5 minutes. Remove meat with a slotted spoon; reserve. Add the yellow onion, celery, sweet pepper, and green onions and sauté until soft but not browned, about 5 minutes. Add the garlic and sauté 1 minute longer. Stir in the beans and their soaking liquid, reserved sausage and ham, parsley, bay leaves, thyme, oregano, and salt, black pepper, cayenne pepper, and Tabasco to taste; be generous with the peppers. Add as much cold water as necessary to cover the beans by about 1 inch. Bring to a boil over medium-high heat; skim off any foam that rises to the top. Reduce the heat to low, and simmer, uncovered, stirring frequently to prevent beans from sticking, until the beans are tender and a thick gravy has formed, about 3 hours. Stir in a little water if the beans begin to get too dry.

Meanwhile, cook the rice as directed on page 15.

To serve, place a scoop of rice in the center of each plate and ladle a generous serving of beans all around. Sprinkle with minced parsley or green onions and serve piping hot.

Serves 4 as a main course, or 6 as a side dish.

Caribbean Chicken and Rice with Pigeon Peas *(Pelau)*

Pilau or *pelau*? Though the spelling and the seasoning changes from island to island, this Caribbean *pilaf* relative has as its common origin Moslems settlers from India. Dried pigeon peas are easier to find than fresh ones, which are sometimes available in Latin American markets. These same markets often carry the peas canned under the Spanish name, *grandules*. If using dried peas, soak them in water to cover overnight, then cook them until tender before starting the dish.

In a cast-iron dutch oven or other large, heavy pot, fry the bacon until crisp. Remove the bacon with a slotted spoon and set aside to drain on paper toweling. Transfer ¼ cup of the bacon drippings to a sauté pan or skillet and reserve. Discard all but 3 tablespoons of the remaining bacon fat.

Heat the rendered bacon fat remaining in the pot over medium-high heat. Add the onion, celery, and sweet pepper and sauté until the vegetables are golden, about 15 minutes. Stir in the chili pepper, garlic, chives, and thyme and sauté 1 minute longer. Add the coconut milk, cooked pigeon peas, and salt and black and cayenne peppers to taste. Reduce the heat to low and simmer for 15 minutes. Remove from heat and reserve.

Add the sugar to the reserved ¼ cup bacon drippings in the sauté pan or skillet and heat over medium heat until the sugar begins to caramelize, stirring constantly to avoid scorching the sugar. Add the chicken pieces and cook, turning frequently, until well browned and almost caramelized all over, 15 to 20 minutes.

Wash and drain the rice as described on page 12.

Add the drained rice to the peas mixture. Stir in the caramelized chicken and the chicken stock or broth. Bring to a boil, then reduce the heat to low, cover the pan, and simmer until the chicken and rice are tender, about 20 minutes. Spoon onto a serving platter, crumble the reserved bacon over the top, garnish with whole chives, and serve.

Serves 8.

1 pound bacon, cut into 2-inch lengths
2 cups chopped yellow onion
2 cups chopped celery, including leaves
1 cup chopped green sweet pepper, membrane and seeds discarded
2 teaspoons minced fresh hot chili peppers, or to taste
2 tablespoons minced or pressed garlic
3 tablespoons chopped fresh chives
1½ tablespoons minced fresh thyme, or 1½ teaspoons dried thyme, crumbled
2½ cups coconut milk (page 16)
4 cups cooked and drained fresh or dried pigeon peas, or 2 cans (16 ounces *each*) pigeon peas, drained
Salt
Freshly ground black pepper
Ground cayenne pepper
3 tablespoons granulated sugar
4 boned and skinned chicken breast halves, cut into large bite-sized pieces
4 boned and skinned chicken thighs, cut into large bite-sized pieces
2 cups long-grain white rice
2 cups homemade chicken stock or canned chicken broth
Whole fresh chives for garnish

Puerto Rican Rice and Chicken Stew (*Asopao de Pollo*)

2 teaspoons minced or pressed garlic
2 teaspoons minced fresh oregano, or
    1 teaspoon dried oregano,
    crumbled
1 teaspoon ground cumin
1 teaspoon salt
1 teaspoon freshly ground black
    pepper
½ teaspoon ground cayenne pepper
6 boned chicken thighs or breast
    halves, skinned if desired
3 tablespoons olive oil or vegetable
    oil, or as needed
1 cup finely chopped onion
1 cup finely chopped green sweet
    pepper
4 ounces flavorful baked ham,
    chopped
1 cup peeled and chopped ripe or
    canned tomatoes with their juices
2 cups white rice
6 cups homemade chicken stock or
    canned chicken broth
½ cup freshly grated dry cheese such
    as Monterey Jack or Parmesan
1 cup cooked shelled fresh green peas
    or thawed frozen petite green
    peas
¼ cup pitted green olives, sliced
1 tablespoon drained small capers
Roasted red sweet pepper or canned
    pimiento, cut into strips,
    for garnish

Very similar to the *arroz con pollo* that's ubiquitous throughout Spanish-speaking countries, except that this version remains soupy, or *asopao*, and is usually eaten with both a fork and a spoon. To make a drier version, cut the liquid by about one-third and leave the chicken pieces whole.

In a small bowl, combine the garlic, oregano, cumin, salt, and black and cayenne peppers. Rub the spice mixture into the chicken pieces and let stand, covered, at room temperature, for 1 hour.

Heat the oil in a cast-iron dutch oven or other heavy casserole over medium-high heat. Add the chicken pieces and sauté until lightly golden, about 10 minutes. Remove the chicken and reserve.

If necessary, add oil to that remaining in the pan to total 2 tablespoons. Add the onion and sweet pepper and sauté until soft but not browned, about 5 minutes. Add the ham and tomatoes and sauté about 5 minutes longer. Return the chicken to the casserole, reduce the heat to low, cover, and simmer until the chicken is tender, about 20 minutes. Transfer the chicken pieces to a cutting surface. When cool enough to handle, cut the chicken into bite-sized pieces; reserve.

Wash and drain the rice as described on page 12.

Increase the heat under the pan to medium-high. Add the drained rice and sauté until all grains are well coated, about 2 minutes. Stir in the stock and bring to a boil. Reduce the heat to low, cover tightly, and simmer until the rice is tender but still soupy, about 17 minutes. Stir in the cheese, peas, olives, capers, and the reserved chicken. Cover and simmer just until the cheese melts and the other additions are heated through, about 5 minutes. Scoop into individual bowls and garnish with the pepper strips.

Serves 6 as a main dish.

Spanish Rice with Shellfish and Meats (*Paella a la Valenciana*)

Add a salad, a loaf of crusty bread, and a bottle of dry white wine and enjoy one of the best rice main dishes on the planet. Vary the shellfish with whatever is fresh and available; sautéed chunks of lobster are especially good.

Heat 2 tablespoons of the olive oil in a *paella* pan or large skillet over medium-high heat. Add the prawns and sauté just until bright pink on the outside and the meat turns opaque, about 3 minutes; remove and reserve. Add olive oil, a little at a time, as needed throughout the rest of the sautéing. Add the squid rings and tentacles and sauté until opaque, 2 to 3 minutes; remove and reserve. Add the pork and sauté until well browned, about 10 minutes; remove and reserve. Add the chicken pieces and sauté until golden, about 10 minutes; remove and reserve. Add the sausage and sauté until browned; remove and reserve.

Reduce heat to medium and pour enough oil into the pan drippings to total about ¼ cup. Add the yellow onion, green onions, and sweet peppers and sauté until very soft and golden, about 15 minutes. Add the garlic, tomatoes, and parsley and cook until liquid has evaporated, about 10 minutes.

Wash and drain the rice as described on page 12. Heat the stock or broth to simmering; reserve.

Add the drained rice to the *paella* pan and sauté until all grains are well coated, about 3 minutes. Add the reserved squid, pork, chicken, and sausage. Stir in the saffron-infused wine, the hot stock or broth, and salt and black pepper to taste. Reduce the heat to low and simmer, gently stirring occasionally, until the liquid is absorbed, about 20 minutes. About 5 minutes before the rice is done, arrange the reserved prawns, clams, and mussels on top.

Remove from the heat and let stand 10 minutes before serving. Garnish with asparagus and sweet pepper strips.

Serves 8 to 10.

Olive oil for sautéing
8 to 10 large prawns, shelled and deveined
1½ pounds squid, cleaned, tentacles separated from bodies, and bodies sliced into ½-inch-wide rings
1 pound lean pork meat, cut into ½-inch cubes
4 boned chicken thighs
4 boned chicken breast halves
1 pound pork sausage, preferably Spanish-style chorizo, sliced into ¼-inch-thick rounds
1½ cups finely chopped yellow onion
6 green onions, including green tops, sliced
2 red sweet peppers, membrane and seeds discarded, cut lengthwise into thin julienne
2 tablespoons minced or pressed garlic
2 cups peeled and chopped ripe or canned tomatoes, drained
¼ cup minced fresh parsley, preferably flat-leaf type
3 cups short-grain white rice
5 cups homemade chicken stock or canned chicken broth
1 teaspoon saffron threads, or ½ teaspoon powdered saffron, or to taste, dissolved in ½ cup dry white wine
Salt
Freshly ground black pepper
24 small clams, scrubbed and steamed until opened
24 mussels, scrubbed, debearded, and steamed until opened
Asparagus tips, cooked crisp-tender, for garnish
Roasted red sweet pepper strips for garnish

Cajun Rice with Pork, Chicken, and Shellfish (Jambalaya)

½ pound Cajun-style andouille or
    other hot smoked pork sausage
4 ounces Cajun-style tasso or other
    smoked ham
Salt
Freshly ground black pepper
1 fryer chicken, cut into serving
    pieces
2 cups long-grain white rice
1½ cups finely chopped yellow onion
1 cup finely chopped celery
1 cup finely chopped green sweet
    pepper
1 bay leaf
1 tablespoon minced fresh thyme,
    or 1 teaspoon dried thyme,
    crumbled
Ground cayenne pepper
2 teaspoons minced or pressed garlic,
    or to taste
2 cups homemade chicken stock or
    canned chicken broth
¾ pound small to medium-sized
    shrimp, peeled and deveined if
    desired
1 pint small or medium-sized oysters
    and their liquid
2 or 3 green onions, including green
    tops, finely chopped, for garnish

Much simpler to prepare than Spanish *paella*, the Cajun version of meats cooked with rice takes its name from the French *jambon*, or "ham," and *ya*, an African word for "rice." These are linked by the Acadian language variation of the French *à la*. During the recent nationwide exploitation of this grand old cuisine of south Louisiana, two restaurants I visited served "jambalaya" that contained not a trace of the grain in what should be a rice dish flavored with meat and sometimes shellfish. Here is an authentic jambalaya based on the way I was taught to cook one by good friend Ed Broussard back home in Louisiana.

Slice the sausage and ham into bite-sized pieces and place them in a cast-iron dutch oven or other deep, heavy pot. Add water to a depth of 1 inch. Cook over medium-high heat until the water boils away, about 10 minutes. Continue cooking until the meat is lightly browned and fat is rendered, about 8 minutes longer. Remove sausage and ham with a slotted spoon and reserve. Leave rendered fat in pot.

Salt and generously pepper the chicken pieces to taste. Cook them in the rendered fat over medium heat until browned, about 6 minutes. Remove and reserve.

Wash and drain the rice as described on page 12.

Add the yellow onion, celery, sweet pepper, bay leaf, thyme, and cayenne pepper to taste (be generous) to the pot and sauté until they are soft, about 5 minutes. Add the garlic and drained rice and stir until rice grains are well coated, about 2 minutes. Add the reserved sausage, ham, and chicken and the stock or broth. Bring to a boil, reduce the heat to low, and stir in the shrimp and oysters and their liquid. Cover and simmer until the liquid is absorbed and the rice is tender, about 20 minutes. Discard the bay leaf and garnish with the chopped green onions.

Serves 4 as a main dish.

Japanese Simmered Beef and Vegetables over Rice (*Sukiyaki Donburi*)

2 cups short-grain white rice

BEEF SUKIYAKI

1½ pound-piece boned tenderloin or other tender cut of beef
½ cup soy sauce, preferably *tamari*
¼ cup *mirin* (sweetened rice wine) or sherry
¾ cup reconstituted *dashi* (fish stock) or homemade beef stock or canned beef broth
3 tablespoons granulated sugar
1 medium-sized yellow onion, halved, then cut into ¼-inch-thick slices
6 green onions, including green tops, cut on the diagonal into 1½-inch lengths
4 ounces fresh *enoki* mushrooms, or cultivated mushrooms, sliced
1 pound fresh *shungiku* (edible chrysanthemum leaves) or spinach, stems removed
1 can (8 ounces) sliced bamboo shoots, drained
1 pound *tofu* (soybean cake), drained and cut into bite-sized cubes
1 can (14 ounces) *shirataki* (yam thread noodles), drained and cut into thirds
4 quail or chicken egg yolks (optional)

Donburi, which translates as "big bowl," is actually a large bowl of rice topped with any one of a wide variety of Japanese meat and vegetable dishes, including *yakitori*, *tempura*, chicken and egg, or, as in this recipe, *sukiyaki*. When the topping is not saucy, a simple mixture of fish, chicken, or meat broth flavored with *mirin* (sweetened rice wine) and soy sauce is usually poured over the top or served on the side for dipping. A favorite lunch in Japan, *donburi* is a good way to use leftover dishes, but the flavor is so delicious it's worth making from scratch.

To begin the *sukiyaki*, trim the fat from the beef and reserve it. Wrap the meat in plastic wrap and place in the freezer for 30 minutes to make slicing easier. Slice as thinly as possible; reserve.

Cook the rice in water as directed rice on page 15, omitting butter and onion.

Combine the soy sauce, *mirin* or sherry, *dashi* or beef stock or broth, and sugar in a small saucepan and stir over medium-high heat until the sugar is dissolved, about 3 minutes; reserve.

Heat a large, heavy skillet over medium-high heat. Rub the bottom of it well with the reserved beef fat; discard fat. Add the meat and cook, turning, just until it is past the pink stage, then push it to one side of the pan. Add the vegetables, *tofu*, *shirataki*, and the reserved soy sauce mixture and cook until the vegetables are crisp-tender, 5 to 7 minutes.

Scoop the hot rice into 4 large individual bowls and top with the *sukiyaki*, including some of the sauce. Crown each bowl with an egg yolk, if desired. Eat with chopsticks.

Serves 4 as a main course.

Chinese Fried Rice

¼ cup sesame seeds
3 cups cold plain cooked rice
About 3 tablespoons peanut oil or
    vegetable oil
3 eggs, beaten
½ cup diagonally cut snow peas
1 cup diced Chinese barbecued pork,
    baked ham, or cooked chicken
1 tablespoon soy sauce, or to taste
1 teaspoon oyster sauce, or to taste
2 green onions, including green tops,
    chopped

This basic recipe for one of the most versatile dishes in the world of rice cuisine can be infinitely varied by substituting ingredients and seasonings according to whim or what's on hand.

Start with rice cooked by your favorite method, or use the recipe on page 15, omitting the butter and onion and using water for the cooking liquid. Most Asian cultures frown on any rice that isn't polished white, but for stir-frying I prefer the nutty taste of brown rice.

Place the sesame seeds in a small, heavy skillet over medium heat and toast, shaking pan or stirring frequently, until lightly golden, about 5 minutes. Pour onto a plate to cool.

Use your fingers to break up the clumps of rice into separate grains; reserve.

Place a wok or large skillet with tall sides over high heat for about 30 seconds. Pour in about 1 tablespoon of the oil and rotate the pan, causing the oil to swirl and coat all the surfaces. Add the beaten eggs. They will immediately set up on the bottom. Slide the solid part to one side to allow the uncooked portion to spread onto the pan and cook. When all the egg has set but is still moist, quickly transfer it to a small bowl and break it up with a fork or slice into thin strips; reserve.

Return the pan to the heat, pour in another tablespoon of oil, and swirl it around the pan. Add the snow peas and stir-fry about 2 minutes. Add the reserved rice, the pork, ham, or chicken, and soy and oyster sauces and stir-fry until all the grains are coated, 2 to 3 minutes longer. Add the reserved cooked egg and the green onions and stir-fry just long enough to heat through. Turn onto a platter, sprinkle with the reserved sesame seeds, and serve immediately.

Serves 4 as a side dish, or 2 as a main course.

Sicilian Stuffed Rice Balls
(*Arancini*)

Translated as "little oranges" because of their shape and finished color, *arancini* make a satisfying snack or a tasty lunch along with a salad.

Wash and drain the rice as directed on page 12.

Combine the saffron and stock or broth in a saucepan over high heat. Add the drained rice and bring to a boil. Stir once, reduce the heat to low, cover, and simmer until the liquid is absorbed and the rice is *al dente* and slightly sticky, about 17 minutes. Remove from heat and cool to room temperature.

Heat the oil in a large sauté pan or skillet over medium-high heat. Add the onion and sauté until soft, about 5 minutes. Add the ground meat and rosemary and sauté until the meat just loses its raw color, about 5 minutes longer. Add the tomato sauce, wine, and peas and cook until the liquid evaporates and the peas are just tender, about 10 minutes longer for fresh peas, or about 5 minutes for thawed. Add salt and pepper to taste.

In a mixing bowl, beat 2 of the eggs. Add the cooled rice and grated cheese and mix thoroughly. Scoop about 3 tablespoons of the rice mixture into the palm of one hand and press it out to form an even round. Place about 1 tablespoon of the meat mixture in the center of the patty, then gently close your hand to encase the filling in the rice. Use both hands to roll the stuffed rice into a ball. Continue making balls until all ingredients are used.

Beat the remaining 2 eggs in a small bowl and pour the bread crumbs into a shallow bowl. Roll each rice ball in the egg to coat completely, then roll in the bread crumbs to cover well. Set aside until all balls are coated.

Pour oil in a deep fryer or saucepan to a depth of 4 inches. Heat to 360° F or until a small piece of bread dropped into the oil turns golden within a few seconds. Carefully drop the rice balls, a few at a time, into the oil and fry, turning frequently, until golden brown all around, about 5 minutes. With a slotted utensil, transfer to paper toweling to drain. If desired, place in a low oven to keep warm until all are cooked. Serve warm.

Makes about 10 *arancini*; serves 4.

2 cups short-grain rice, preferably arborio
½ teaspoon saffron threads, crumbled, or ¼ teaspoon powdered saffron
1 quart homemade chicken stock or canned chicken broth
2 tablespoons olive oil, preferably extra-virgin
½ cup finely chopped yellow onion
¼ pound lean ground pork or beef
1 teaspoon minced fresh rosemary, or ½ teaspoon dried rosemary, crumbled
¼ cup fresh or canned tomato sauce
¼ cup dry white wine
⅓ cup shelled fresh green peas or thawed frozen petite green peas
Salt
Freshly ground black pepper
4 eggs
½ cup freshly grated pecorino or Parmesan cheese
About 1½ cups very fine dried bread crumbs, made from Italian or French bread
Olive oil or vegetable oil for deep-frying

Cajun Rice-and-Pork Sausage
(Boudin Blanc)

Expect the casings to break open as the sausage cooks. I find it more appealing to discard the casings after cooking and spoon the creamy, highly spiced stuffing onto warmed plates.

Soak the casing in warm water until soft; reserve.

Cook the rice in chicken stock as directed on page 15, omitting the butter and onion.

In a large, heavy saucepan, combine the pork, pork fat, yellow onion, green onions, garlic, parsley, bay leaves, thyme, sage, mace, allspice, salt, peppers, cream, and water. Bring to a boil over high heat, then reduce the heat to low and simmer, stirring frequently, for 10 minutes. Remove from the heat and stir in the warm rice. Mix thoroughly, then drain in a colander and cool to room temperature.

Drain the casing. With a sausage-stuffing cone or large funnel, stuff casings with the pork mixture to form sausages about 6 inches long, tying off links with cotton string as you go. Wrap tightly and refrigerate for up to 4 days, or freeze for up to 3 months.

To cook, place the sausages in a heavy skillet or sauté pan in which they fit comfortably. Add about ¼ cup cold water, place over low heat or in a preheated 325° F oven, and cook until piping hot, about 20 minutes, turning several times to prevent sticking. Add a few tablespoons of water as necessary. Alternatively, cook in the microwave for 1 minute.

Serves 8.

About 1¾ yards fresh small hog or sheep sausage casing (available at butcher shops)
1 cup long-grain white rice
1½ cups homemade chicken stock or canned broth
1½ pounds fresh lean pork shoulder, ground or finely chopped
1½ pounds fresh pork fat, ground or finely chopped
1 cup finely chopped yellow onion
4 green onions, including green tops, finely chopped
1½ tablespoons minced or pressed garlic
¼ cup minced fresh parsley, preferably flat-leaf type
2 bay leaves, finely crumbled
1 tablespoon minced fresh thyme, or 1 teaspoon dried thyme, crumbled
1 tablespoon minced fresh sage, or 1 teaspoon dried sage, crumbled
¼ teaspoon ground mace
⅛ teaspoon ground allspice
1 tablespoon salt, or to taste
2 teaspoons ground cayenne pepper, or to taste
1 teaspoon freshly ground black pepper, or to taste
1 cup heavy (whipping) cream
⅓ cup water

Indonesian Rice Dinner *(Rijsttafel)*

Pork Sate (recipe follows)
Coconut Shrimp (recipe follows)
Condiments (see introduction)
3 cups long-grain white rice

The Indonesian feast the Dutch call a *rijsttafel*, which simply means "rice table," takes its name from the large plate of rice that is served to each diner. The rice is the centerpiece for the up to two dozen dishes offered at such an affair. Limited space allows for only two recipes to get you started, but other possibilities include kabobs, curries, stir-fried vegetables, spiced baked fish, or any main dish reminiscent of the Indo-Malayan archipelago. This fare also features a host of condiments such as freshly grated coconut, chutneys, fiery relishes, cooling cucumbers, chopped nuts, sliced tropical fruits, and fried bananas.

Prepare the main dishes according to the recipes that follow, adding several recipes of your own, if desired.

Cook the rice in water as directed on page 15, omitting the butter and onion.

To serve, arrange the main dishes and condiments on the table or buffet. Provide each guest with a plate on which rice has been spread evenly to create the "table."

Serves 8.

→

Pork Sate for *Rijsttafel*

2 pounds lean pork, thinly sliced

MARINADE
1 tablespoon jaggery (palm sugar) or
    brown sugar
1 tablespoon curry powder
2 tablespoons crunchy peanut butter
½ cup soy sauce
½ cup freshly squeezed lime juice
2 teaspoons minced or pressed garlic
Ground cayenne pepper

PEANUT SAUCE
1 tablespoon vegetable oil
1½ tablespoons minced shallot
1½ tablespoons minced or pressed
    garlic
1 tablespoon minced fresh ginger root
⅔ cup crunchy peanut butter
½ cup coconut milk (page 16)
2 teaspoons jaggery (palm sugar) or
    brown sugar
1½ teaspoons soy sauce
1 tablespoon freshly squeezed
    lime juice
Ground cayenne pepper

Grated lime zest for garnish
Fresh cilantro (coriander) sprigs
    for garnish

The sauce and marinated pork can be prepared as long as a day ahead, then grilled just before serving.

Thread the pork onto bamboo skewers.

To make the marinade, combine the sugar, curry powder, peanut butter, soy sauce, lime juice, garlic, and cayenne pepper to taste in a large shallow bowl. Add the skewered pork and marinate at room temperature for at least 2 hours, or in the refrigerator as long as overnight for a more intense flavor.

To make the sauce, heat the oil in a pan over medium heat, add the shallot, garlic, and ginger and sauté until soft but not browned, about 2 minutes. Add the peanut butter, coconut milk, sugar, soy sauce, lime juice, and cayenne pepper to taste. Cook, stirring constantly, until the mixture is well blended and thickened. Remove from the heat and let cool. If a very smooth sauce is desired, transfer to a food processor or blender and purée. Reserve.

Prepare a moderate charcoal fire in an open grill or preheat the broiler. Remove the skewered pork from the marinade, reserving the marinade.

Cook the skewered pork, turning several times and basting with the marinade, over medium-hot coals (or under a broiler) until crispy on the outside but still moist inside, about 5 minutes. Sprinkle with lime zest and garnish with cilantro sprigs. Serve with the room-temperature peanut sauce.

Serves 8 as part of a *rijsttafel* meal.

Coconut Shrimp for *Rijsttafel*

Heat 2 tablespoons of the oil in a skillet over medium heat, add the garlic and chili, and sauté until soft but not browned, about 2 minutes. Remove from the heat, let cool, then combine with the coconut milk, lime juice and zest, and salt to taste in a bowl. Add the shrimp, rubbing with your fingers to coat all surfaces. Cover and marinate, refrigerated, for 2 to 4 hours; remove from the refrigerator about 15 minutes before cooking.

Heat the remaining 2 tablespoons of the oil in a wok or skillet. Add the shrimp and marinade and stir-fry just until bright pink on the outside and the meat turns opaque, about 3 minutes. Remove to a platter, sprinkle with the toasted coconut, and serve immediately.

Serves 8 as part of a *rijsttafel* meal.

¼ cup safflower or other high-quality vegetable oil
2 tablespoons minced or pressed garlic
1 teaspoon minced fresh chili pepper
½ cup coconut milk (page 16)
2 tablespoons freshly squeezed lime juice
1½ teaspoons grated lime zest
Salt
1½ pounds large shrimp, shelled and deveined if desired
Grated fresh or dried coconut, lightly toasted

Indian Chicken and Rice Casserole
(Murghi Biryani)

The crowning glory of India's rice cookery, *biryani* can be made with lamb, pork, seafood, or mixed vegetables. During the cooking some of the rice will turn bright golden while other grains will remain sparkling white. Serve with a relish of chopped fresh tomato, onion, cucumber, cilantro, lemon juice, cumin, and cayenne pepper.

Wash and drain the rice as described on page 12.

In a large bowl, combine the drained rice with enough cold water to cover, stir in 1 tablespoon salt, and let stand for at least 3 hours or as long as overnight.

Combine the saffron and cream or milk in a small bowl and let stand for 3 hours.

In a food processor or blender, combine the onion, garlic, ginger, 3 tablespoons of the almonds, and 3 tablespoons water and blend until smooth. Reserve.

Heat the butter in a small skillet over medium heat. Add the remaining 2 tablespoons almonds and cook until golden, about 4 minutes. Transfer to paper toweling to drain; reserve.

Heat ¼ cup of the oil in a skillet over medium-high heat. Drop the raisins into the oil and remove with a slotted spoon as soon as they plump, just a few seconds. Transfer to paper toweling to drain; reserve.

Add 2 more tablespoons of oil to the same skillet. Add the chicken pieces, a few at a time, and brown on all sides. Transfer chicken pieces to a bowl once they are browned. Reserve.

2 cups long-grain white rice, preferably basmati
Salt
1 teaspoon saffron threads, or ½ teaspoon powdered saffron
2 tablespoons heavy (whipping) cream or milk, warmed
1½ cups finely chopped yellow onion
4 garlic cloves
1-inch-piece fresh ginger root, peeled and coarsely chopped
5 tablespoons slivered blanched almonds
1 tablespoon unsalted butter
¾ cup vegetable oil
¼ cup golden raisins
1½ pounds boned and skinned chicken breasts and thighs
1 cup plain yogurt
1 teaspoon ground cinnamon
1 teaspoon ground cloves
1 teaspoon ground coriander
½ teaspoon ground cardamom
½ teaspoon freshly grated nutmeg
Freshly ground white pepper

→

Add the remaining 6 tablespoons oil to the same skillet. When heated, add the reserved onion paste and cook, stirring constantly, until lightly browned, about 5 minutes, adding a little water if the mixture begins to stick to the pan. Slowly add the yogurt, about 1 tablespoon at a time, whisking or stirring vigorously to blend. Return the chicken and any accumulated juices to the pan. Add ½ cup water and bring to a boil. Reduce the heat to low, cover, and simmer for 20 minutes. Stir in the spices and salt and white pepper to taste and simmer until the chicken is tender, about 5 minutes longer. Remove from the heat and cool just until the chicken can be cut into bite-sized pieces.

Preheat the oven to 300° F.

In a large stockpot, bring 4 quarts water to a rolling boil over high heat. Add a generous sprinkle of salt. Drain the rice, rinse, and drain again. Slowly add the rice to the boiling water. Return to a rolling boil and cook for 6 minutes. Drain the rice immediately.

Spread about one-third of the rice on the bottom of an ovenproof casserole. Cover with about half of the chicken mixture, then spread with half of the remaining rice. Cover with the rest of the chicken and top with the remaining rice. Drizzle the reserved saffron cream or milk over the top. Cover tightly with foil, then a lid, and bake until steaming hot, about 30 minutes.

To serve, sprinkle the top of the *biryani* with the fried raisins and the butter-fried almonds.

Serves 6 as a main dish.

Creole Rice Fritters *(Calas)*

¾ cup long-grain white rice
2¼ cups cold water
1½ teaspoons salt
1½ packages (¼ ounce *each*) active
    dry yeast
¾ cup warm water
⅓ cup granulated sugar
1½ teaspoons ground cinnamon
1½ teaspoons freshly grated nutmeg
1¾ cups plus 2 tablespoons
    unbleached all-purpose flour
4 eggs, well beaten
Vegetable oil for deep frying
Powdered sugar for dusting
Strawberry jam or Louisiana dark
    cane syrup

Gone are the days when the call *Belle cala! Tout chard!* ("Lovely rice! Piping hot!") could be heard wafting through the New Orleans French Quarter, as black cooks roamed the streets selling these yeast-raised, deep-fried rice cakes. Traditionally served at breakfast, *calas*, a name taken from an African word for rice, also make a wonderful afternoon treat or homey supper dessert. Instead of deep frying, thin the mixture with a little milk and cook on a griddle as you would pancakes.

Wash and drain rice as described on page 12.

In a large, heavy saucepan, combine the drained rice, water, and salt and bring to a boil over high heat. Stir once, reduce the heat to low, cover, and simmer until the rice is very soft, about 25 minutes. Drain off any excess water.

Transfer the rice to a large bowl. Mash the rice with a wooden spoon to break up kernels, then cool to room temperature.

Dissolve the yeast in the warm water, then add it to the rice, stirring to combine thoroughly. Cover with plastic wrap or foil and set in a warm place to rise overnight.

In the morning, add the sugar, cinnamon, nutmeg, flour, and eggs to the rice. Beat well to combine, then set in a warm place to rise for 30 minutes.

Pour the oil into a deep fryer or saucepan to a depth of 3 inches. Heat the oil to 375° F, or until a small piece of bread dropped into the oil turns golden in a few seconds. Preheat the oven to 200° F.

For each fritter, drop about 1 tablespoon of the soft dough into the hot oil. Cook only a few fritters at a time, turning frequently to brown evenly until the puffs are golden brown and crusty. Remove with a slotted spoon and drain on paper toweling in the warm oven while you fry the remaining batter. Dust with powdered sugar and serve hot with dollops of strawberry jam or drizzled with cane syrup.

Serves 8.

American Rice Pudding with Strawberry Sauce

1 cup short-grain rice, cooled slightly
3 eggs, lightly beaten
1 cup heavy (whipping) cream
1 cup milk
2 tablespoons unsalted butter, melted
½ cup granulated sugar
1 teaspoon vanilla extract
½ cup golden raisins
½ teaspoon freshly grated nutmeg

STRAWBERRY SAUCE
2 cups fresh strawberries, hulled
Granulated sugar

This old-fashioned southern pudding remains one of my favorite desserts, with or without the new-fangled sauce.

Cook the rice in water as directed on page 15, omitting butter and onion. Remove from heat and cool slightly.

Preheat the oven to 325° F.

Combine the cooked rice, eggs, cream, milk, butter, sugar, vanilla extract, raisins, and nutmeg. Turn into a buttered 2-inch-deep, 8-inch-square baking dish and bake until set, about 40 minutes, stirring every 10 minutes.

To make the sauce, purée the strawberries in a food processor or blender. If desired, push through a wire sieve to remove seeds. Place in a small saucepan, add sugar to taste, and heat gently over medium-low heat until warmed.

Serve the pudding warm or at room temperature with the warm sauce.

Serves 6 to 8.

Mexican Rice Pudding
(Arroz Con Leche)

1½ cups short-grain white rice
2 2-inch cinnamon sticks
Zest of 1 lime or lemon, removed
    in 1 piece
3 cups water
¼ teaspoon salt
1 quart whole milk
2 cups evaporated milk
1¼ cups granulated sugar
½ cup raisins
4 egg yolks, lightly beaten
1 teaspoon vanilla extract
2 tablespoons unsalted butter,
    cut into small pieces
Ground cinnamon

The essence of lime is captured in this rendition of Mexican rice pudding, a dessert that's almost as popular as the country's famous flan. It has become my favorite rice dessert.

Best served warm, this delectable pudding should still be a bit soft or soupy when served. It is also good at room temperature, and any leftovers can be mixed with milk and reheated for breakfast.

Wash and drain the rice as described on page 12.

Combine the cinnamon sticks and lime or lemon zest with water in a medium-sized saucepan. Bring to a boil over medium-high heat, then add the drained rice and salt and stir once. Cover, reduce the heat to low, and simmer until the rice is tender and all the liquid is absorbed.

Add the whole milk, evaporated milk, sugar, and raisins and stir well. Increase the heat to medium and cook, stirring frequently, just until the mixture begins to thicken, about 20 minutes, or longer if you desire a thicker pudding. Remove from the heat and discard the lime or lemon zest. Stir about 3 tablespoons of the hot pudding mixture into the beaten egg yolks. Stir the egg mixture and the vanilla into the pudding.

Preheat the broiler.

Turn the pudding into a shallow flameproof serving dish, dot with the butter, and sprinkle with cinnamon to taste. Place the pudding under the broiler just until the top begins to brown lightly, about 3 minutes. Serve immediately or at room temperature.

Serves 8 to 10.

VARIATION: Eliminate cinnamon sticks. Substitute orange or grapefruit zest for the lemon or lime and add a pinch of saffron to the milk. Sprinkle the top of the pudding with brown sugar and freshly grated nutmeg before broiling.

Indian Rice Pudding *(Kheer)*

The perfumelike fragrance of roses adds enchantment to this typical Indian pudding. Very similar recipes are found in Middle Eastern cuisines. To duplicate the opulent presentation shown, spoon the pudding into a full-blown pesticide-free rose and sprinkle it with shavings of edible 24-karat gold leaf, available at art supply stores.

Wash, soak, and drain the rice as described on page 12.

In a medium-sized saucepan, combine the drained rice and 1½ cups water. Bring to a boil over medium-high heat, reduce the heat to low, cover tightly, and simmer until the water is absorbed, about 10 to 12 minutes.

In a large saucepan, combine the rice with the light cream or half-and-half, sugar, and cardamom. Bring to a boil over medium-high heat, then reduce the heat to low, and simmer, uncovered, until the liquid is absorbed, about 1 hour, stirring frequently to prevent the rice from sticking to the bottom of the pot. Remove from the heat, transfer to a serving bowl, and cool to room temperature. Stir in the rosewater and most of the pistachios, reserving some for garnish.

Serve at room temperature or cover and chill. Garnish with pistachios and rose petals, if desired.

Serves 8.

1 cup long-grain white rice,
  preferably basmati
1½ cups water
2 quarts light cream or half-and-half
1 cup granulated sugar
½ teaspoon ground cardamom
2 teaspoons rosewater, or to taste
  (optional)
½ cup chopped pistachios for garnish
Pesticide-free rose petals for garnish
  (optional)

Filipino Rice Squares
(Bibingkang Malagkit)

Glutinous rice teams with long-grain rice in this dense pudding topped with brown sugar and peanuts.

Wash, soak, and drain the glutinous rice as described on pages 12 and 18. Wash and drain the long-grain rice as described on page 12. Combine the two rices in a bowl, add hot water to cover, and let stand 10 minutes. Drain.

If using canned coconut milk, do not shake before opening. Spoon off 2 cups of the thick coconut cream from the top and reserve. If using fresh coconut milk, chill, then reserve 2 cups of the thick cream.

In a large, heavy saucepan, combine the rice, 4 cups of the coconut milk, the granulated sugar, and salt. Bring to a boil over medium-high heat, then reduce the heat to low, cover tightly, and simmer until the rice is tender but not mushy, about 30 minutes. Transfer to a greased 9-by-13-inch baking pan, pressing with your fingers to flatten the top of the rice and make it even. Reserve.

Preheat the oven to 375° F.

In a saucepan, combine the reserved coconut cream, the brown sugar, vanilla, and ground peanuts. Cook over medium-high heat until the sugar is dissolved and the syrup is thickened, about 5 minutes. Gradually stir about 3 tablespoons of the syrup into the beaten eggs, then pour the eggs into the syrup in the saucepan and cook, stirring constantly, until slightly thickened, about 1 minute. Pour evenly over the rice.

Bake until set, about 30 minutes. Remove from the oven and cool to room temperature. Garnish with peanuts and cut into squares to serve.

Serves 12.

2½ cups white glutinous rice
½ cup long-grain white rice
Hot water
6 cups coconut milk (page 16)
1 cup granulated sugar
½ teaspoon salt
2 cups packed brown sugar
1 teaspoon vanilla extract
½ cup ground unsalted roasted
    peanuts
3 eggs, lightly beaten
Unsalted roasted peanuts for garnish

Southeast Asian Sticky Rice

INDONESIAN STICKY RICE
(Bubor Ketan Hitam)
1 cup black glutinous rice
5 cups water, or as needed
4 ounces jaggery (palm sugar),
    broken into small pieces, or 1 cup
    packed brown sugar
Coconut milk (page 16)

**THAI STICKY RICE WITH
MANGOES** *(Mamuang Kao Nieo)*
1½ cups white glutinous rice
1⅓ cups coconut milk (page 16)
½ cup jaggery (palm sugar) or
    granulated sugar
½ teaspoon salt
4 or 5 ripe mangoes
Coconut cream (page 16) for topping
    (optional)

These two recipes for sticky rice use similar ingredients, except for the color of the rice. Indonesians transform a black variety of glutinous rice into a traditional thick breakfast porridge that also makes an unusual dessert. Pass coconut milk for topping at the table.

Street vendors in Thailand sell white sticky rice steeped in coconut milk as a special treat during mango season. Try it with more plentiful summer peaches or nectarines.

Wash, soak, and drain the rice as described on pages 12 and 18.

In a large saucepan, combine the drained rice with 5 cups water and the sugar. Bring to a boil over medium-high heat, then reduce the heat to low, cover tightly, and simmer for 30 minutes. Uncover and continue to cook, stirring frequently, until the rice is quite soft, about 1 hour longer. Add more water during cooking if necessary.

To serve, ladle the porridge into bowls. Top with coconut milk at the table.

Serves 4.

Cook the rice as directed on pages 12 and 18.

In a saucepan, combine the coconut milk, sugar, and salt and stir over medium-high heat until the sugar is dissolved, about 3 minutes. Pour over the warm rice in a mixing bowl, stir to combine, and let stand, uncovered, for 30 minutes.

Peel the mangoes and cut each half from their large stones. Slice each half into 4 long pieces. Arrange pieces on individual plates and add a scoop of the rice. Top with some of the thick coconut cream, if available. Serve immediately or refrigerate for up to 1 hour.

Serves 6.

Sicilian Black Rice Cake
(Torta di Riso Nero)

This unusual gooey cake, inspired by a Marcella Hazan recipe, is even tastier with a scoop of wine custard. Sicilian cooks use candied citron instead of the crystalized ginger I prefer.

To make the cake, wash and drain the rice as described on page 12.

Combine the drained rice and pine nuts or almonds in a saucepan. Add the sugar, salt, half-and-half, and brewed coffee. Bring to a boil over medium-low heat and cook, stirring frequently, until the rice is very tender, the liquid is completely absorbed, and the mixture is thick, about 45 minutes to 1 hour; add a little more half-and-half during cooking if liquid is absorbed before rice is tender. Remove from the heat and stir in the ground coffee beans, chocolate, ginger, lemon zest, and butter and mix thoroughly until the butter is melted.

Generously grease a 9-inch springform cake pan with butter. Spoon the rice mixture into the pan, pressing with your hands to create a layer of uniform thickness. Cover tightly with plastic wrap and refrigerate at least 24 hours or as long as 3 days.

To make the wine custard, combine the egg yolks and sugar in the top pan of a double boiler and beat with a wire whisk until frothy. Add the Marsala, white wine, brandy, if using, salt, and lemon and orange zests. Place over simmering water and beat continuously until the custard is thickened and smooth. Transfer top boiler pan from heat to a bowl of ice cubes to cool.

Fold the whipped cream into the cold custard with a rubber spatula. Chill for at least 2 hours or as long as overnight.

Remove the cake from the pan and transfer to a serving plate. Garnish with some of the the chilled custard and the crystalized ginger, citrus zest, and violets. Serve slightly chilled or at room temperature. Pass the remaining custard at the table.

Serves 8.

BLACK RICE CAKE
¾ cup short-grain white rice
1¼ cups (about 6 ounces) pine nuts or blanched almonds, finely chopped
1 cup granulated sugar
⅛ teaspoon salt
4½ cups half-and-half, or as needed
2 cups brewed espresso or other strong dark coffee
1 tablespoon finely ground espresso or other dark-roast coffee bean
4 ounces bittersweet chocolate, finely chopped
½ cup chopped crystalized ginger (about 2 ounces), or to taste
Minced or grated zest (with no bitter white pith) of 2 lemons
2 tablespoons unsalted butter
Unsalted butter for greasing pan

CHILLED WINE CUSTARD
2 egg yolks
¼ cup plus 2 tablespoons granulated sugar
½ cup Marsala wine
¼ cup dry white wine
1 tablespoon brandy (optional)
¼ teaspoon salt
1 tablespoon minced lemon zest
2 teaspoons minced orange zest
1 cup whipping cream

Crystalized ginger pieces for garnish
Crystalized citrus zest for garnish
Candied violets for garnish

Rice Cooler *(Horchata de Arroz)*

2 cups white rice
1 cup (about 4 ounces) blanched
    almonds
3 tablespoons ground cinnamon
2 quarts milk, warmed, or hot water
¾ cup granulated sugar, or to taste
1 teaspoon vanilla extract
Ice cubes

Popular in Central America as well as Spain, this refreshing summer beverage deserves to become better known north of the border. I find that when the rice is steeped in milk rather than water the final result is tastier. Covered and refrigerated, the cooler keeps up to a week. Top it off with a splash of Kahlúa, if you enjoy the liqueur.

Wash and drain the rice as described on page 12.

In a large bowl, combine the drained rice, almonds, and cinnamon with the warm milk or water and soak at least 6 hours, or preferably overnight. Drain, reserving liquid.

Purée half the rice-almond mixture in a food processor or blender. Add about 1 cup of the reserved liquid and blend until as smooth as possible. Transfer the blended mixture to a bowl and repeat with the remaining rice mixture and liquid.

Strain the mixture through 3 layers of dampened cheesecloth into a glass pitcher or jar, squeezing the cloth to extract all the milky liquid. Stir in the sugar and vanilla. Chill and serve over ice cubes.

Makes about 2 quarts.

VARIATION: For a chocolate-flavored drink, add about ¼ cup sweetened cocoa powder, or to taste, to the rice and almonds.

Index

Recipe Index

Acknowledgments

To everyone at Chronicle Books for the fine work in editing, printing, distributing, and promoting my work. It's wonderful to realize this makes nine books we've done together.

To William Goulet, director of public relations, Gump's, San Francisco, for the loan of china, crystal, silver, and linens. And to his assistant, Pam Franklin, for her extraordinary help and patience in selecting the beautiful props.

To Patricia Brabant for sharing so completely her creative genius and transforming my cooking into glorious color. As one reviewer wrote, "she should teach the class in salivary gland stimulation." And to her assistant Edy Owen for a very skillful job in keeping the studio going.

To my studio kitchen assistant, Gail High, for all her chopping, stirring, storing, cleaning, errand running, recipe sharing, and for keeping us all amused with her lively tales of life with teenagers.

To Stephen Suzman for his ideas and beautiful roses.

To my sister, Martha McNair, for her generous styling assistance in the photo studio.

To Cleve Gallat and Peter Linato of CTA Graphics for once again translating my designs and words into beautiful finished pages.

To my associates Addie Prey, Buster Booroo, Joshua J. Chew, Michael T. Wigglebutt, and Dweasel Pickle, who stood or laid by throughout the production of this book and who relished a ton of leftover rice.

To my family and friends who offer a continual backup system of assistance and encouragement.

And, as always, to my best friend and partner, Lin Cotton, for his unwavering belief in me and too often unsung assistance in countless ways.